ALASKAN BUSH
ADVENTURES

ALASKAN BUSH ADVENTURES

Lessons from the Land
Lessons from the Lord

Don Ernst

ELM HILL

A Division of
HarperCollins Christian Publishing

www.elmhillbooks.com

Alaskan Bush Adventures

Lessons from the Land
Lessons from the Lord

Published in Nashville, Tennessee, by Elm Hill, an imprint of Thomas Nelson. Elm Hill and Thomas Nelson are registered trademarks of HarperCollins Christian Publishing, Inc.

Elm Hill titles may be purchased in bulk for educational, business, fund-raising, or sales promotional use. For information, please e-mail SpecialMarkets@ ThomasNelson.com.

All Scripture quotations, unless otherwise indicated, are taken from the Holy Bible, New International Version*, NIV*. Copyright © 1973, 1978, 1984, 2011 by Biblica, Inc.* Used by permission of Zondervan. All rights reserved worldwide. www.Zondervan. com. The "NIV" and "New International Version" are trademarks registered in the United States Patent and Trademark Office by Biblica, Inc.*

Library of Congress Cataloging-in-Publication Data

Library of Congress Control Number: 2018962329

ISBN 978-1-400306121 (Paperback)
ISBN 978-1-400306213 (Hardbound)
ISBN 978-1-400306220 (eBook)

CONTENTS

THE GREAT
HUNTING PLAN

It was cold outside—I mean cold! It was −50°F and dark. The darkness was lasting twenty hours every day. Winter had come. But it was warm sitting beside the blazing woodstove and the lights shone brightly inside the house. That evening, my son-in-law and his family had walked over for a visit. It is in such times when plans are made. One day, the sun will be shining brightly again and the temperature will rise above freezing, and with that change of season the ducks and geese will be back. So it was in this setting that a new plan was being formed for the coming spring waterfowl season.

Every spring and fall there is an area a few miles upriver where the geese tend to congregate. In this particular section of river the snow melts early, exposing the sandbar that contains new shoots of vegetation. The small stems of willows on the bank form a backdrop and offer some protection. In the spring, the challenge is being able to get to that area since the main river is normally still clogged with ice. "So how are you figuring that we will be able to get to this hunting area?" It seemed like a legitimate question that I asked my son-in-law.

He then began explaining this new, great hunting plan.

"At the edge of the village, where the slough makes a turn to the north, just beyond the beaver dam, that will be our starting point. We will put your canoe in there. From there we can paddle to where this slough connects into another, larger slough. Once we reach that point we can follow the slough for a while, then portage the canoe over to a series of lakes. Once we have paddled through the lakes we can portage a little distance to where the hunting area is by the river. Then after the hunt, we will just reverse our course and head back home." He continued, "It won't be bad. It's only going to be about five miles each way, most of it by canoe."

Well, that sure seemed like a great plan to me. I liked the idea of sitting in the canoe and paddling for most of the trip and only having to portage the canoe a couple of short distances. The plan was formed and set. Now it was just a matter of waiting for spring and the birds.

In due time, spring returned to the land—and with it the geese. We were greeted with a clear sky the morning my son-in-law and I lowered the canoe into the slough. The forecast called for calm winds and warm temperatures. This was going to be an exciting hunt. No one else had yet been to this particular hunting area, as the ice still held its grip on the river. We were undoubtedly going to be the first ones to reach this country. After putting all the gear in the canoe, we pushed it off the bank and into the water, barely making a wake. The canoe was a cedar strip canoe that I had made a few years back, roughly seventeen feet long. It would carry a good load without settling much into the water.

The paddling was easy, even somewhat relaxing, as we made our way down the narrow slough. The plan that had been made during the depth of winter was now unfolding before us. "What is that ahead of us?" I asked, fearful of knowing what the answer would be. Sure enough the ice hadn't melted in this part of the slough. No worries—we will just portage around this little chunk of ice, get back in the slough, and be on our way. A minor setback, but it was all working according to plan. Back on the slough again we began paddling. Unfortunately, we only went a short distance and there it was again—ice all the way across the slough. As we climbed the bank and looked down the slough, all we could see was snow and ice where we had planned that there would be water. Plan A was not working out so well. Not to be deterred, we quickly came up with Plan B. Carry the canoe to the next slough, put it in there, and paddle to the lakes.

We dragged the canoe up the bank, put the paddles in, and carried it to the next slough. This was going to take a little longer than we planned and for sure required a little more work. But in our minds, we could just see all the geese on the sandbar. Onward we went! In time we reached the other slough. You got to be kidding me. As we looked in amazement at the next slough, all we saw was ice—nothing but ice. Plan B just ended. How could such a great hunting plan begin to unravel so quickly? Though we were dismayed, we came up with Plan C. Continue to portage the canoe over to the lakes. There we would put in and paddle to the river.

By this time the sun was shining brightly and it was starting to get warm. Sweat was beginning to flow from our bodies as we pushed on. We were going to get to the river later than planned, but fortunately the days were long now. After a while we came to the first lake and there was water. Unfortunately, the water was only along the very edges and not near enough to launch the canoe. This was unbelievable! Plan D: get out some ropes, tie them to the canoe, and drag the canoe to the next lake. Along the way we had the opportunity to shoot a few ducks. It didn't seem like a few ducks could add so much weight to the canoe, but there was definitely a noticeable difference. After portaging for a long way, parting the weeds and grass as we went, there in the distance was an awful sound—gunshots.

While we had started our trip on one end of the village, two other guys had started their hunting trip from the other end of the village. Their trip had begun on the river. Little did we know that the ice went out on the river through the night. These two men traveled upriver in a little boat and made it to the hunting area. The gunshots we heard were coming from these two men. They were hunting the same geese. Plan E...turn the canoe around, once again wrap the ropes back over our shoulders, and begin retracing our steps, dragging the canoe back to the village. Some hours later, sweaty and exhausted, we made it back home. Our great hunting plan, schemed in the winter, turned out to be nothing more than a grueling workout. Obviously, things had not even come close to what we had planned.

There is an account in the Old Testament, recording what seemed like a reasonable plan. I can enjoy the countryside as I make the trip, or so he thought. Joseph obediently followed his father's direction and headed off to find his brothers. Little did he know what was about to happen. Upon finding his brothers and approaching them, he quickly became aware of their intent to harm him. From the account recorded in Scripture we know that he was put in a cistern, and shortly thereafter sold as a slave. What had seemed like a simple little journey was now going to lead to years of incredible trials. This was not what Joseph had as his Plan A. However, God was going to use Joseph to save His people. It was God's plan (Genesis 37:12–36).

We find a similar situation later in Scripture. There were the chores to do—the cooking, and the cleaning. But life was good for Esther. After all, Mordecai had taken her in as his own daughter when her father and mother had died. Little did she know what was about to happen. Shortly, she would find herself in the harem of the king in the citadel of Susa. In time, the king would set up Esther as queen. Later in the account it was Esther who went before the king. Even though she might be killed for going before the king without being invited, she took the risk. It was Esther who stood before the king, spoke up, and saved her people, the Jews. This was not Esther's plan, but it was God's plan for Esther (Esther 2:1–4:16).

How many times do we make plans as we go through life? In our way of thinking they may even be great plans, such as our geese-hunting plan. However, they are exactly that: *our* plans. We may have several plans in life, but only God's sovereign plan is what will last. Scripture reminds us in Jeremiah 29:11: "For I know the plans I have for you," declares the Lord, "plans to prosper you and not to harm you, plans to give you a hope and a future." Perhaps, instead of focusing so much on our plans, we should take time to seek what plans the Lord may have for us. In the end, His plans are always better than ours—with or without geese to bring home.

ARE WE
ACCOUNTABLE?

"**D**o you realize what the penalty is for illegally transporting a firearm through Canada?" the border agent asked me.

"Not exactly, but I have looked at the requirements for bringing a gun into Canada," was my answer.

"This rifle is the only firearm that you are bringing into the country?"

"Yes," I replied. The guard was clear and straightforward with his questions, and I was just as straightforward with my answers.

One of the responsibilities of a missionary is to update your supporters, whether they be financial or prayer supporters. As a missionary we are accountable to them. One way to report to them is to send out newsletters, updating them on how the ministry is progressing. Another method is visiting them in person. In light of this responsibility, every four years we make a trip to the lower forty-eight to visit these supporters. We decided that for this trip we were going to drive to the mainland, going through Canada. All the preparations had been made, appointments were scheduled, and the trip details were finalized.

We packed our suitcases and flew from the village into Fairbanks. We were running behind schedule as it had taken a little longer finalizing the details and getting out of the village. We parked the plane, transferred the luggage to the car, and started burning up the pavement. It is always a great road trip and so we were looking forward to it. Since it covers a lot of miles it is a good opportunity to have some quiet time.

One of the activities that I planned while we were in the lower forty-eight was to hunt in Colorado where we used to live. Because of this hunt I had brought a rifle. Knowing we would cross through Canada I researched the requirements for transporting a rifle through their country. As we approached the Canadian border crossing, I was glad I had done the research concerning rifles. I pulled up to the gatehouse and the guard asked me if I had any guns. I informed him that I had a rifle. I took the gun into the guard station, filled out the papers, paid the fees, and headed down the road.

Driving through Canada is always amazing. The scenery is beautiful, the people are friendly, and there are plenty of uncrowded roads. Normally the trip for us takes about three days before we cross back into the United States. As we approached the U.S. border station, I showed them the paperwork I had attained for going through Canada. Also, upon being asked, I informed them about the rifle I was carrying. Everything went smoothly through both border crossings and we made our way down the road. I had a settled feeling as we entered back into our own country.

The next day we were driving through Big Sky country, Montana. As we were traveling down the road, my wife asked an interesting question. "Do you have your flight bag with you?"

I forgot I had put the bag behind her front seat in all the hurry to get on the road. I looked and there it was behind her front seat. There were too many important items in that flight bag for me to misplace it because it contained all my flight charts, my logbook, cables, and satellite phone. I breathed a sigh of relief to know we had it—but it was short lived. My wife asked the next interesting question.

"Do you have your pistol in the flight bag?"

I was stunned. Of course, I had my pistol in the bag. I always carry that pistol as part of my survival gear in the plane while flying around bush Alaska.

I was all too aware, after having inquired about the gun regulations for Canada, that it is illegal to transport a pistol through Canada. I had violated the law, even be it unknowingly. I had crossed through two border crossings, had my vehicle searched, and failed to declare my pistol. I am sure the Canadian border patrol agent, if he had found the pistol, would have confiscated it. If we would have wrecked while still in Canada and the pistol discovered, I could have been put in jail. After the fact and knowing the possibilities that could have happened, I was simply glad to be driving as a free man in Big Sky country.

I unknowingly escaped a tough situation on our trip through Canada—my wife might had been making the trip all on her own. There are people today who also think they will escape having to pay any consequences for their actions. According to their thinking, they can either justify what they do or justify why they shouldn't face any judgement. How many times does one hear the comment "God is a God of love, therefore He will not let anyone go to Hell." In their thinking, they reason that there probably isn't even a Hell. If all else fails, according to their accounting, their good outweighs their bad. However, God is a jealous God and a righteous judge—He does not judge according to man's thinking or standards, but rather His standards. These standards are given to us in His word.

This was not the first time that crossing through the Canadian border had brought this lesson home to me. The first time I crossed the border I was younger and with the whole family. We were excited, though apprehensive, for all the unknown, as we were heading to Alaska for the first time. It was the start of answering the call of the Lord to do mission work in bush Alaska. We said good-bye to friends and had an auction to sell everything before we left Colorado. The supplies we did need to take with us we loaded into a horse trailer and piled the family into the old Ford station wagon. In those days the Ford was actually made out of metal and could easily handle the trailer. There was plenty of room for the three kids in the back of the station wagon. Back then there were no seat belt laws so the kids could rotate between sitting in the seat or playing games in the back. The trip was going smoothly for all the miles and all the bodies, and after a few days we were ready to cross into Canada.

It was a little chilly at the end of March as we worked our way north. We were excited for our first trip into Canada, and as we were drawing close to the border crossing I was nervous since we had so much stuff with us. I hoped we wouldn't have to unload the horse trailer for inspection. I pulled up to the guard station and stopped. Nobody came out right away, so we waited, but still no guard appeared. There on the other side of the guard station was a big parking area. I figured it would be a good idea to pull ahead and park in that parking area to get out of the way. But it was not a good idea. Someone quickly exited the guard station and came our direction. They wondered what in the world I was doing and asked if I noticed the stop sign. They thought it might be a good idea for us to visit them in the guard station. Now I was nervous.

The border patrol agent proceeded to take the whole family into the guard station. He placed the family in one room and me in a separate room. After visiting with me and asking some rather thorough questions, I was reunited with my family. He did the same process with my wife, but after two hours we were all reunited and given permission to continue. Back together and breathing a sigh of relieve, we were escorted back to the vehicle. The last thing the agent told me was, "Stop at the stop sign."

Through all of that ordeal I was reminded that there are consequences for your actions. You are accountable, whether or not you think so. God also makes it clear in His Word that we all are accountable—we are accountable to Him no matter what we think. Romans 14:12 says we will give an account of ourselves to God, and Hebrews 4:13 again reinforces that teaching: "Nothing is hidden from God." No one is excused, for everyone must give an accounting to God. If we are accountable to God, we need to understand to which standards we are held accountable. Maybe it would be a good idea for us to look at God' standards—those written in Scripture. This is something we need to wrestle through. No sin is hidden from the Lord, just like my pistol behind the seat. When we disobey His clearly marked signs, the Word of God, we have only ourselves to blame. We must forget our erroneous thinking. Rather turn to God and His standards. Only then, when we stand accountable before our Maker, we will not stand before Him trembling in fear.

ARE YOU
AVAILABLE?

Once again we were leaving the cold, dark days of winter behind. We were bound for sunny skies, warm temperatures, and clear, blue ocean water—Mexico—Cancun, Mexico to be exact. When our son moved to Mexico and married a local girl he apologized for living so far from home. We reassured him that anywhere is far away from Alaska. They served for some years now as missionaries in that part of the world. Every year we venture down there to visit and do Bible teaching. The reality is that the schedule normally doesn't allow for much leisure time, but the family and fellowship are great.

When we were recently in Cancun visiting, I had the opportunity to do some teaching at the YWAM (Youth With a Mission) base. Most of the students were local Mexicans from some of the surrounding region. Using a translator, I did a Bible series for them before they headed out to do their outreach trip. While there I learned that some of the thinking within the local Mexican culture promotes the idea that only college-educated individuals can do ministry. Also, the only real ministry is done on Sunday mornings, the preaching of God's Word. That concept was foreign to me, but that was the mind-set in this culture.

However, sometimes I wonder if certain aspects of that thinking are even in our Western culture. How many times have I heard the statement while attending a church service, "Well, that's the preacher's job. He can go visit, or he can share the gospel with that individual—that's what we pay him for." The individual may then proceed to explain that he isn't qualified to do that or doesn't know enough. Perhaps Americans aren't much different than Mexicans—we turn to the individual who is schooled and trained to do the "ministry" and we sit in the pew.

What of the twelve apostles? These were men whom Christ called, ultimately to take the gospel to the uttermost parts of the world. If you were going to entrust such an incredible undertaking to some individuals, what kind of men would you look for? In today's world, in our culture, it would be men who have degrees, with letters after their names. Perhaps men with great experience, which would give credibility that there would be success in the mission. Is that the kind of men whom Christ called to be His apostles? Hardly.

Now that isn't to say that men of training could not have been apostles. Some were trained, but not all. Half of the disciples whom Christ called were fishermen by trade, and one was even a dreaded tax collector. They were hands-on kind of people. Maybe not knowledgeable in some circles but experts in their trade. These were the men who, with their hands, provided for individuals. Years of experience had made these men who they were. But in the end, would these be the men whom you would entrust with a mission for the world? Not just any mission, but the greatest mission known to man—proclaiming the gospel of Jesus Christ. This mission would have an eternal message, giving truth to one's eternal destiny. Are these the men whom you would turn to and whom you would count on?

"You got this. My hands are off the controls and it's all you." "Push the throttle completely in and keep the airplane down the middle of the runway." "You can do this." Those were the words from my old flight instructor. As I sat strapped in with the seat belt around me, I nervously pushed the throttle in and we began to roll down the runway. The little Cessna began to build up speed and the torque of the engine began to pull the airplane to the left. The instructor told me to put in right rudder, but I panicked and put in left rudder. Needless to say, we quickly exited off the left side of the runway into the grass. Carefully the instructor put in right rudder and got us back on the runway. He reassured me I could do this. After continuing down the runway a short distance we were airborne. What an amazing experience for the first time. Not perfect, but mission accomplished.

When Christ first started gathering disciples, the apostles had issues. There in the boat, a familiar setting for them, they feared for their lives in the midst of the storm (Matthew 8:23–26). Send them home—that was the disciple's thinking because there was not enough food for so many people. We only have five loaves and two fish—what can we do? (Matthew 14:13–21). We tried, Jesus, but we could not drive the demon out of the boy. However, Jesus had the boy brought to him and merely spoke and the demon was driven out of the boy (Matthew 17:14–21). These are a few examples, there are others, indicating that the apostles were in a growing relationship with Jesus. There was still room for spiritual growth. Yet in time, Jesus would leave and the ministry would be entrusted to these men.

The time came when Jesus ascended before their very eyes and went back to His heavenly home. After receiving the promised Holy Spirit, these men stood before the crowds and began to proclaim the gospel of Jesus Christ. The disciples spoke, men and women responded, and the church grew by thousands. In the midst of all that was happening, the people noted that these were unschooled, ordinary men—however, these men had been with Jesus (Acts 4:13). These men with emboldened faith, a servant's heart, and a passion for the gospel continued the work that Jesus started before their very eyes.

I wondered, *What do we need today to continue the mission of proclaiming Christ to the world? What is it that will make the greatest difference in getting the gospel message out and bring men to Jesus? What needs to happen in my own life that I might be like the first apostles? What is it? Do I need to have more years of walking with Jesus? Do I need more education? Do I need to understand Greek a little better?*

Well, I do not know all the answers for that. But there are three lessons we can learn from the apostles who walked before us.

First, we need a complete, unwavering faith in Jesus. No matter the setting and no matter the situation, nothing will cause us to lose faith or to lose hope. We must put complete trust in Him. Everything we need, everything we have is in Him and not us. My faith must be grounded in the Rock.

Second, we need to proclaim God's Word and not our own. His words are truth and stand forever, and are powerful. We have a testimony to share of what God has done for us and what he continues to do. But our words pale in comparison to His. May it be more of Him and less of us.

And third, this world is not about us—it's about Him. If we can grasp what it means to be a servant of God just as the apostles, would it change our lives? What does this world offer? Why does this world have such a hold on us? Why should the temporary things of this world consume us rather than the things of eternity? We need to switch our thinking, change our hearts, and understand that He comes first in life. We need to become His servant, first and foremost, and nothing else should be number one in our lives.

With unwavering faith, with the words of God and with a servant's heart, these twelve men proclaimed the gospel with a heart of passion. They knew and experienced what Jesus had done for them and they could not contain this message within themselves. If we were to walk in the same manner as the apostles, we would proclaim His message with passion. May there be no topic, no thinking, nor any message more important than the message of the cross. The cross confronts and divides, but it gives life if we choose. This is our message.

Could it be that more than anything else, what we need is what the apostles had? Is this what we need today in our life and for this world? We need an unwavering faith to share God's truth as servants with a heart of passion for the lost world. Any disciple is capable of this. The more important question is whether you are available to be used by God. Are you?

ARE YOU KIDDING?

"Would you be interested in helping me pack out a moose?" I asked my son-in-law.

Of course he felt obligated to help, even though he was working a construction job at the time. "How far do we have to pack it?"

That was the question I had hoped he wouldn't ask. "Well, I would guess it to be about a quarter mile, maybe a third mile, possibly half a mile or so back off the riverbank." I could just imagine him wondering if I was kidding, since we normally get a moose close to the water's edge. Unfortunately, this wasn't a joke.

It had been a tough hunting season. We were not seeing many moose even though we had spent a lot of time in the field. During those dry times of not seeing any moose you start to get a little nervous. You know you need that meat to live on because there are no meat markets or super-markets in the bush of Alaska. Hours are spent boating along the river, hoping to find a moose feeding along the edge of the willows. Stopping frequently, you walk back into the meadows and call—all in an effort to find that elusive bull moose. Even though the season is three and a half weeks long, you start counting the days you have left when it's a tough season. It was in this setting that my wife and I set out early one morning to hunt once again.

Dawn was breaking as we loaded up the boat. With fuel and gear onboard, we headed upriver. The air was cool early in the morning this time of year, as attested to by the frost on the landscape. I was glad that I had built a small cab for the boat, which was much warmer than sitting out in the open. As we traveled miles and miles upriver we didn't see anything. Empty meadows and no sounds. This was becoming all too familiar. After traveling upriver for roughly thirty miles, we nudged the boat onto the bank. We were headed back into one of our favorite meadows, which had been productive in the past. Still there was nothing. There was no sound, no sign, and no moose. We went back to the boat feeling discouraged again. Going only slightly farther upriver, we again tied the boat to the bank and headed up to another large meadow.

Scanning the meadow and its edges with binoculars didn't reveal anything—but wait! Was that a bull making a call? The morning air was still, which meant sounds could be picked up easier. We listened intently and there it was again—a bull was calling from over on the left side of the meadow. We worked our way closer to the edge of the brush, peeking out into the meadow. Shielded by some of the last brush, I began to make a moose call. I tried a bull call and then even a cow call. The bull started responding and suddenly we could see him step into the meadow. We called back and forth, and with each sequence the bull slowly made his way in our direction. The brush shielded us, and even though the grass was dying it still stood over three feet tall and also aided in hiding us.

Time seemed to slowly pass as we watched the bull work his way toward us. Once he got one hundred and fifty yards out, he stopped. Then he turned broadside to us and started to walk past us. Sensing that he was not going to get any closer I decided to take the shot. The roar and kick from the .45-70 was both heard and felt. The bullet hit its mark. Immediately, the bull started to run and I took one more shot, and then he turned and ran directly away from us. It was amazing how much country a moose can cover in a short timespan. My wife and I watched as he entered the brush on the far side of the meadow and exited the meadow for the last time.

Knowing that I had hit the moose, we visually marked the spot where the moose exited the meadow. Walking through the tall grass we went to the spot where he had turned away from us and started heading out of the meadow. Following his trail through the grass, we reached the far edge of the meadow. Shortly after we entered the scattered brush we found the bull. The shot had been good. In relief and excitement my wife turned to me and started to give me a high five. My hand did not go up to meet hers in the air.

"Aren't you excited?" my wife asked.

My response to her was straightforward. "Look how far we have to pack." I was thinking to myself, *Why did it have to run so far back?* The ground the moose covered in less than a minute now translated into hours of hard work. I was grateful to have a moose and to know we had meat for the winter. However, this was no small moose. The rack was over sixty inches and it probably weighed around fifteen hundred pounds. We were going to have to pack roughly eight hundred pounds of meat back the half mile to the river.

My wife and I couldn't hardly even move the moose, let alone cut it all up by ourselves. We marked the spot, went back to the boat, and headed to the village. I knew that we would need help and that's why I was now visiting with my son-in-law. A plan was made, supplies gathered, and back up the river we went with two more men to help in the cutting and packing process. As we all ventured back to the downed moose and they saw the distance we had to pack, they all agreed that I wasn't kidding about the distance. With everyone working hard we finished in a few hours, climbed back in the boat, and headed for the village.

Likewise, I wonder what Aaron thought when Moses was up on the mountain and the people gathered around him and asked him to make them gods that would go before them. Did Aaron basically say, "You got to be kidding me, after all that God has done for us?" No. Rather, Aaron told the people to bring him their pieces of gold and he would make a golden calf that would be their god (Exodus 32:1–4). How could they so quickly abandon their God? This was the God who freed them from slavery and the God who provided their every need as they journeyed to the Promised Land. This was the God who was willing to continually forgive them when they were disobedient and rebelled. This was the God who was faithful in all His promises. And this was the God of the heavenly realms—not the earthly gods of men. Despite what he knew was right, Aaron began melting the gold to make a calf.

Is not the God of Aaron and the Israelites the same God over us? Do we ever lose sight of God as the Israelites did and then look to the world? Are we like them? "You've got to be kidding me," you might retort. Yet so many times we make friends with the world rather than choose the work of obedience. In James 4:4, it is written: "You adulterous people, don't you know that friendship with the world means enmity against God? Therefore, anyone who chooses to be a friend of the world becomes an enemy of God." That is exactly what the Israelites did while Moses was on the mountain. They left God and turned to the thinking and the things of the world. Have you ever noticed that if you look closely at the thinking and the teaching of the world, you'll see that it runs opposite of what God says? No wonder James wrote that friendship with the world is hatred toward God.

John also wrote, "Do not love the world or anything in the world. If anyone loves the world, the love for the Father is not in them. For everything in the world—the lust of the flesh, the lust of his eyes, and the pride of life—comes not from the Father but from the world" (1 John 2:15–16). Just as James was clear and adamant regarding the world and God, so also John pointed out the differences in very clear writing. We need to guard ourselves because it's so easy to be caught up in the world and lose sight of the One who died for us and gave us life and instructions on how to live that life. No one said it would be easy not to follow the world. It wasn't easy to pack out the moose. But it was worth it. And it will be worth it, for eternity, to follow God and His ways, not that of the world's. I am not kidding.

Do I Know You?

There was no wind, the sun was shining brightly, and the temperatures were warm for May in this part of Ohio. The three of us stood at the edge of the lake, enjoying the day. The one girl I knew, but I had no clue who the other girl was. The girl I knew mentioned that the water looked so inviting it made her want to go swimming. Well, I was brought up with the mind-set that you should try to help people and give them what they want or need. What a perfect time to put that upbringing into practice. With one graceful movement I swept the girl up in my arms and threw her into the lake. If swimming is what you want, then swimming is what you'll get. The girl who I didn't know looked at me horrified and began to take some steps back away from me and the water. Meanwhile the girl in the water, though shocked, made her way back up to the edge of the lake. Standing there, completely soaked, she admitted that the water did feel good.

Shortly after that incident I needed a person to work for me during the summer months. I contacted the girl I knew and she indicated she was already committed to another job. However, her girlfriend was not working. With some hesitation, I contacted the unknown girl and asked if she would be interested in working for me that summer. After the lake incident earlier that month, I didn't think she would say yes—but she did. This was the beginning of a great working relationship that lasted through the summer. As the weeks progressed this girl began to take on a new fascination for me. She was becoming more than just an employee—she started to get a hold on me.

By the end of summer I finally asked her out on a date. "Do you think you would be interested in going frog gigging with me?" This girl was something else! She said she would go even though she didn't know exactly what frog gigging was. That Saturday night we put the little john-boat in the creek with paddles and a light and spear in hand. We were set to try to get some bullfrogs. By the end of the trip we were planning a meal of frog legs together as I took her back home. Though I didn't know her, just a few months ago, I now knew she was the girl for me. Approximately a year later we were married. Thinking back on those memories, I realize that was just the beginning of the stories we would make together—stories that are forty years in the making and still continuing. Sometimes it is hard to imagine that it all started with a girl I did not know.

Awhile back, there was an interesting conversation that took place between another man and a woman, recorded in John 4. The woman had no clue who the man was. She was going about her daily activity, and at this time of the day she would draw water from a well. But this was not just any well—it was Jacob's well. This well had history and was dug centuries ago. Yet it was a good well and the water still flowed through the ground. People would go to the well for water—for livestock and for themselves. This water was refreshing as one dealt with the dry heat of the day. This woman went to the well just as usual that day.

It was not the normal time when most people would go to the well—but it was the time of day this Samaritan woman went. One could speculate why the woman went at noon, but in any event this was her chosen time. At that time Jesus was sitting by the well, tired from His journey and possibly from the heat of the day. As the woman was drawing near to the well, she saw a man sitting there. When she reached the well something strange transpired—this man began talking to her. But this wasn't just any man—he was Jewish. It was not appropriate for any man to talk to her, but even more inappropriate by a Jewish man. One might wonder if she thought, *Do I know you? What do you think you are doing?*

Jesus asks her point-blank, "Will you give me a drink?" It was a logical question. It was hot and Jesus had walked a long way, and was tired and thirsty. This was a well; it had water. Jesus needed a drink and she had a jar. Little did the woman know that the conversation was about to turn.

Then it happened—Jesus made a natural transition. In a moment he shifted the conversation from the physical need of water to the spiritual need of living water. As the conversation unfolded, Jesus was able to declare who he was and the gift of the Father. This Samaritan woman came to recognize her need for this living water, and Scripture recorded that she put her faith in Christ. Then, because of her testimony, people from the village came to listen to Christ and they also put their faith in Him.

Early on in our village ministry, I was trying to connect with the men. Men are always a challenge when it comes to spiritual things. Women and children respond to the gospel—but most men seem to check out. Knowing that they would not be coming to church, I thought of how I could meet with them on their own turf. As I was walking around the village one winter, I noticed a common scene—men were continually working on their snowmobiles. It didn't matter what the temperature was or the weather conditions, they would be working on their machine. There was no way I would want to work on my machine outside when the temperature was well below zero. With cold metal parts and cold tools, this all meant freezing-cold hands. I tried to think of a solution.

In time I came up with a plan. I harvested some dead spruce trees, milled them into building materials, and made a shop. Traveling by snowmobile, I was able to find a stand of trees to harvest, and slowly, one by one, the logs piled up by my neighbor's mill. In time I began to make the building material and then constructed the shop. I put a sloping ramp on the front of the shop and lined it up with two three-foot doors. With this setup a person could drive their snowmobile right into the shop. Shortly, the structure was completed and tools were in place. The shop immediately became a magnet for guys who wanted to work on their machines.

Part of my winter days were now spent answering the phone and letting the person know when there should be room in the shop for his snowmobile. The shop was about six hundred square feet. Between my woodworking tools and mechanic tools, I could get three snowmobiles in at one time. Word of the shop quickly spread to other villages. Sometimes there would be a knock on the door and someone traveling through who needed some work on their machine would ask if they could use my shop. Many people I didn't know beforehand, I was able to get to know after we visited in the shop together. One advantage for me was that as I watched people work on their machine, I learned a lot more about snowmobiles.

I reached my goal. I found a way to connect with men—on their turf and in a comfortable setting. Remembering how Jesus took the subject of water and turned it into a spiritual outreach, so became my desire for the shop. I was able to take that setting and use it to help turn conversations into a spiritual direction. The opportunities came, even with some people I did not know. Standing over a machine and looking at a carburetor that wasn't running properly because the needle setting was out of sync was redirected to communicating that in our own life there are physical needs. But in the same way there are spiritual needs, and if they are not balanced properly then problems arise. Through the years the shop ministry became the most effective tool to reach out to the men.

There are needs all around us and people in need of a Savior. Many of these people we do not know, but we need to be like Christ—we need to find a way to connect with them, then find a way to turn the conversation to the call to Christ. These people could be people at school, at work, or just someone we bump into. That first meeting with an unknown girl by the lake led to a lifetime of being together. As we visit and share with someone, even someone we don't know, may they get to know the Lord Jesus and spend eternity with Him.

DO YOU HAVE AN ANCHOR?

*D*id the rope break? The anchors ripped out of the ground? When I woke up in the middle of the night, those were my first thoughts. It was obvious the storm had hit full force since the wind was howling through the small cove of the lake. Though I was groggy, I wondered why the houseboat was moving around so much.

Just two days earlier I stood in the small marina on the lake. The owner of the business handed me the final paperwork that I needed to complete for the houseboat rental agreement. As he examined the documents he gave me a strange look and asked, "So how many people are going to be on the houseboat?"

"There will be my wife and I," was my reply.

The marina guy glanced back in my direction and reminded me that this was almost a sixty-foot houseboat. "You are telling me that there is just going to be the two of you?"

Without hesitation I let him know once again that there would only be the two of us. We were about to have a relaxing vacation on Lake Mead in Arizona. Another missionary lady was watching our kids for us in the village and we were going to celebrate our twentieth wedding anniversary on the lake, in the houseboat. We were looking forward to the quiet time—no phone calls, no people constantly in our home, and

23

no daily responsibilities. This would be the first time that we would celebrate an anniversary and we were going to make the most of it.

We had left the village with frost on the ground and cool temperature in the air. Winter was coming quickly to our region of Alaska. Arriving at Lake Mead, we were in our short-sleeved shirts as the sun was warm in the clear, blue skies. Before arriving at the lake, we had the taxi driver stop by a grocery store. We loaded up on all the foods that were hard to come by in the village—fresh fruits, lettuce, tomato, and good beef. I was going to put the grill to good use. Finally, we loaded all the supplies and our gear onto the houseboat. The marina guy gave us our final instructions and we were on our way. The lake was huge and we were ready to explore.

The houseboat was incredible! There were all the cooking facilities you needed—fresh water, plenty of sleeping accommodations, and two steering consoles. You could sit on the main deck and look out a big glass sliding door as you steered, or you could go to the upper deck and steer from an open cockpit. Since the summer season was over, the lake was empty of its normal activities and we were going to spend most of our time on the lake during the weekdays. We sat on the upper deck, enjoying the view of all the stars under a clear sky with no lights and no noise. This was just the end of our first day and we were ready to go hike and explore some more country the next day.

Weather can change quickly—at least that was the case for us on the second day. Apparently, there would be a strong cold front pushing down from the north. This front would cause strong winds, but no moisture was expected. The wind began to pick up during the day and so we found a small cove to beach the houseboat and spend the night there. Between the location and the anchor system, it looked like we would be okay. The anchor system consisted of two one-inch rebar that were three-feet long, which were then driven crisscross into the ground. There was an anchor system for each side of the houseboat. We beached the houseboat, set up the anchors in the ground, tied it all securely, and began to wait out the storm.

Throughout the night the wind began to grow in intensity. The sky was still clear and the moon was shining down, but the wind was howling. Later in the night when I woke up, I could sense the houseboat was moving way too much. Panic set in as I was afraid that something went wrong and that we were adrift in the huge lake. We got up and began shining our lights on the shore; we could see that the anchors were almost ripped out of the ground. The last thing I needed was for the boat to break free. I knew the anchors would just be dragged into the lake and the wind would drive the boat at will. The wind might push the boat into the rocks, or out into the lake—all of this without daylight to help me save the boat. Frantically, I started up the engine while my wife used forward thrust to hold the boat against the bank, and I scrambled to shore and with the aid of a light and sledge in hand, I was able to reinstall the anchors in the ground to secure the boat. Dawn came after the restless night, and with it the passing of the main storm front. The winds began to slow down and we could relax again. The anchor system, though it was good, was not fail proof. Fortunately, we woke up in time to save the houseboat.

This was probably a small wind in comparison to what the disciples experienced in the boat with Jesus. A furious storm came upon them while on a lake and waves were crashing over the boat. These were experienced fishermen—men who had been through other storms. But this storm had them scared. The oars wouldn't help, and if they had an anchor it was useless, too. They, in their own strength, could do nothing. They turned to their only hope in their desperate situation—the Lord Jesus. He would have to save them—He would be their anchor in the midst of the storm. Jesus rebuked the wind and the storm ceased (Matthew 8:23–27). What about us as we go through life and we face our own storms? Who do we have as an anchor? The water reminds us of the importance of anchors.

Some days seem to run together. Flying kids to Bible camp in the summer is one of those times. This day was no different than any other camp day—prepare the float plane for all the flying, pump the floats, fuel the plane, and do the preflight inspection. While I do this, my wife lines up the flying schedule and makes sure all the kids are ready to board the plane on time. With all the flying that needs to be done, the schedule gets very tight. Normally, I bring kids from our village and from a couple of the surrounding villages to the camp. The kids love the camp and it's a time of great activity and good Bible teaching.

Hauling three to five kids, depending on size, each trip into camp with up to ten hours of flying per day makes for the full schedule. Each time I go into camp, the staff is there to meet me, welcome the kids into camp, and bring me fuel for the plane. After a long day of flying, the staff encouraged me to visit awhile and have a snack with them. After some discussion, I finally agreed to take a small break before heading home. Once I land on the river with my floats, I taxi to the bank, rotate the plane around, and drag the tails of the floats unto the riverbank. Then I tie the plane to the bank with it facing out so it's ready to taxi out for takeoff.

With the plane on the bank, I agreed to go up to the dining hall for a little break. After a short visit and a few snacks, I headed back to the river to head home. As I approached the bank a fearful sensation started to come over me. I would normally see the plane by now, but as I got closer to the edge of the bank, I noticed my plane was gone. Panic set in. I ran down the steep bank to the water's edge and looked downriver—there, floating along with the current half a mile downriver, was my yellow floatplane. I knew there was a good chance for some serious consequences. What if the wing slammed into the steep river bank and was damaged? What if I couldn't find a way to go downriver to get the plane quick enough to save it? Frantically I looked for a solution. I decided to jump into a boat and race downstream, but as I turned the key to start the boat, nothing happened. Then the camp staff person remembered that they had taken the battery out of this boat to be used in another boat. What else could go wrong? I looked downstream again and the plane was slowly meandering downriver, with the current carrying it along.

I looked on up the shore and I saw a canoe. This was going to have to be my rescue vehicle. A camp counselor and myself piled into the canoe and began paddling downstream. The whole time I kept watching the plane, hoping that it would not collide with the bank. After paddling for a long time, we pulled up beside the floats of the plane. We climbed onto the floats and tied the canoe to them. Then we stepped into the plane, started the engine, and taxied back to the camp. I was grateful nothing was damaged on the plane and thankful for the help—I was relieved that it was only my pride that took a hit.

Why did all this happen? I was tired and unfocused on the task at hand and had forgotten to use my rope to anchor the plane to the bank. That lack of an anchor, though only for a brief time, almost caused major damage to my float plane. In a similar way, I can go through life and if I don't keep my spiritual anchor in place, I can bring major problems upon myself. What if I begin to wander from the ways of God? What if I get off the path He has called me to? My fellowship with Him will be broken, and possibly with other believers, as well. Satan will begin to distract me and draw me away and drag me down. I need to remember that Christ is my anchor. Hebrews 6:19 reminds me that He is my hope and that He is my anchor. Family, friends, money, job, position are never secure—only Christ is secure. He is my hope. He is unchanging. He is my strength. In the storms of life, I need to be like the disciples and learn the lesson—I need to be reminded that my hope, my anchor, is in Christ.

He has given me His word and He will give me strength in time of need. He will give me grace for the situations I face. He will always be with me and never leave me. He will, as promised, be my unfailing anchor in life.

Do You Have The Answer?

Sometimes life can have exciting moments. Some of these events you are aware of and approach with great anticipation. Sometimes we are not aware of what is about to happen and are caught by surprise. As a believer, we are reminded in 1 Peter 3:15 to always be ready to give an answer for the hope that we have, whatever the situation—to live a life that will bring with it the anticipation of being able to give someone the answer that we have found for eternal life.

We live in the far northern part of the Alaskan interior. With the middle of winter, it should be cold—it was cold. Temperatures were well below zero. In these temperatures it makes everything in life more complicated. Things begin to break and it's a struggle to keep things warm, like the house and even yourself. During these days it becomes a time to focus on the essentials of life, and one such essential is food.

With the nearest road being 250 miles away, stores are not right around the corner. Providing for your own needs is a basic principle of life in the bush, and that is why a subsistence lifestyle is the norm. With that lifestyle comes the necessity of putting meat on the table. Alaska has abundant natural resources from which people can draw upon to meet these needs. In our region you can go under the surface of the water and tap into fish. On the surface you tap into birds like ducks and geese. And on the land there is moose, caribou, or bear.

This winter, and for this family, the quarry was going to be moose. Given the time of year and location this was the best option. This family needed meat in a desperate way. Even though the temperature was brutal, the need would override the elements. Leaving the cabin on a snowmobile she left her elderly parents behind, hoping to find a moose quickly. She had everything she needed for the hunt—a rifle, some food, boy's axe, and extra supplies. From the cabin she began to weave her way up the mountain, making a trail as she went. At least going up the mountain and climbing higher brought warmth. It is always interesting how one doesn't need to gain much altitude to see the temperature rise—this is because warm air is thinner and rises, while cold air is heavier and settles in the low country.

Roaming the mountain netted no sign of game. Turning the snowmobile around, she decided to head for the lower country. Country that was much flatter and hopefully contained some moose. The downside to this would be the fact that the temperature would be considerably colder, maybe by twenty degrees. The hunt would continue. But then it happened—an event that held potential tragedy.

The call came by radio. The report from the elder couple stated that their daughter had gone out to harvest a moose for them; however, she had not returned home. It was her second day out and they were worried for her. Could the village send out a search-and-rescue team to try to find her? It was too late to start the day the message was received, but it would give the team time to organize and get a good start the next day. This time of year, the days are short regarding light, and the sun would be up for roughly three hours with a little dusky light on each side of that. Even during the day, the sun would barely make it above the tree line.

Morning came, the search team had been organized, and they were ready to implement their plan. Everyone was a little nervous. This would be the third day out for the girl and the temperature in the village was around forty below zero. It would probably be fifty below in the search area. There was reason for concern as the searchers headed out on snow-mobiles. It would be a long ride to the area, roughly fifty miles away. Once there, they would have to figure out where she might be.

I have seen planes have mechanical breakdowns when the temperature starts getting really cold. Because of this, I had come up with my own personal operating guidelines. At twenty below zero I would check to see how important the flight would be. If it was not essential, I would wait for warmer weather. If the flight was important I would proceed. However, once the temperature dropped to thirty below I would cancel any flying. It was not just a mechanical situation, but also the reality that if something happened in flight that required an emergency landing, I would be back on the ground in thirty below zero weather—possibly with injuries.

It was forty below and the search team had asked if I would be will-ing to fly. This could be a matter of life and death. I agreed to make the flight. I asked an elder to accompany me since I wanted his wisdom and experience, both in the search and if we experienced any plane trouble. The plane had been preheated, fueled, and readied for the flight. Bundled up to keep warm, the two of us climbed into the Cessna 180 and departed the village. It had been arranged with the search-and-rescue team that if we saw anything we could contact them on the marine band radio.

After half an hour we flew over the cabin. Immediately, we could see her snowmobile trail leave the cabin and head up the mountain. We decided the best option was to follow her trail, wherever it may lead. Up the mountain we saw the trail going between the trees and steadily upward. Then it suddenly turned and started back down. The trail broke out of the timber and into more open flats and headed off in a northerly direction. As we flew, we focused intently on the trail. It was chilly in the plane. But I kept thinking how cold it was down below—cold for her and cold for the search-and-rescue team making its way out to the search area. Would we be able to find her? And if we did, what condition would she be in?

As we were flying with our eyes intently searching for anything that would give us a clue to her whereabouts, the elder spotted something to the right. There it was, a small plume of smoke rising up with an almost bluish tint. I turned the airplane in that direction and, as we approached the area, I began flying closer to the ground. There she was. The fire was small, but we could see her by it. We circled over her a couple of times and then began to climb. I gained some altitude to be able to communicate with the search team. We were able to contact the ground team and give them our observation and the GPS coordinates where she was located. With a great sigh of relief we turned the airplane home toward the village.

On our way home we talked about the fact that neither one of us had seen the snowmobile. Arriving back at the village we were able to give a good report. The search team on the ground made their way out to the girl. It took a couple more hours for them to reach her after they had received our report, but after reaching her they worked their way back to the elder couple's cabin. The search team spent the night at the cabin since light was fading. It was also a good place for them to warm up and rest.

When the search team made it home to the village the next day, we were able to get a few more details of what happened to the girl. Apparently, she was crossing a small slough and broke through the ice. The snow machine went into the water and she couldn't get it out. She had gathered wood, grabbed the last of her rations, and set up under a few trees. During the ordeal and on the last day, she had partially fallen through the slough and got wet as she was trying to gather wood. She had also broken her boy's axe, possibly due to the handle being brittle with the extreme cold. When the team found her, she was down to just a few crackers and a partial jar of jam.

It became apparent that if she had not been prepared she probably would not have survived her ordeal. This would beg the question of whether I am prepared spiritually. Am I ready to give an answer if someone asks me for the reason my life is different and the hope I have? Jesus gave His last command, saying we should make disciples. The first step in making disciples is to share the gospel. Can I clearly take the Word of God and share the truth of His saving grace? Am I prepared?

DON'T MISS THE MARK

During the summertime, my wife and I would enjoy getting in the boat and heading out on the river. It didn't matter whether we were gathering wood for the winter or getting punk for the gnat season. Punk is a fungus that grows on birch trees and when you put it in a fire it slowly smolders, which helps drive away the bothersome gnats. In the village where we lived, the gnats were horrendous so we were always excited for the first few freezes in the fall since it killed off the gnats. Whatever the reason, getting on the river was always a chance to get a break, have a little quiet time, and enjoy the scenery. Traveling around each bend brought an expectation of seeing something exciting, like a cow and calf moose swimming across the water or swans taking to flight or a beaver swimming into his house. There was always a special draw to the river.

One of the activities we did as a family on the river in the fall was to go duck hunting. One fall we all piled in the boat and started our duck-hunting adventure. I normally drove the boat while my grandsons were the gunners. There was a reason why I always liked to be the driver—I had to be one of the worst shotgun shooters in the village, well, maybe not just the village. It seemed like it didn't matter what I tried, I just couldn't seem to hit the ducks. My son-in-law would say which way he thought I missed the bird. He would let me know whether he thought I shot over them or behind them, and sometimes I have no idea. It was so bad that out of a box of twenty-five shells if I got two birds I was having a good hunt. That made for some expensive duck meat. Between the teasing and the expense, driving the boat seemed a good option.

We continued up the small river, following it as it twisted around the landscape. The trees were displaying their fall colors. The white birch bark with the contrasting yellow leaves interspersed among the green spruce trees was awesome. There wasn't any wind and so the river was calm, and the water was reflecting everything. The blue sky, the trees... it was an amazing sight. What also made it special was that is was a nice warm day—something we don't always get in the autumn. As we made our way up the river, the grandsons were having success. It seemed so easy for them to bag a duck. After a while, and with much persuasion, I agreed to be a gunner. The pressure was on. How can I let my young grandsons outgun me? No matter how hard I tried, the end result was always the same—shot after shot resulted in no duck. The only thing I consistently got while duck hunting was a sore shoulder.

Then it happened. A misguided duck accidentally flew into my shotgun pattern. I wounded it so it turned and flew downriver, but I had him in sight. We went down to where the duck landed and I saw it swimming. We were close and so I lined the duck up with the bead on the shotgun and fired off a round. The sight was incredible! The water exploded with the impact of the steel shot. Water, seemingly everywhere, flew several feet into the air. Finally, the water settled back down and, to my amazement, there was the duck, still swimming. I couldn't even kill a swimming duck. Although it seemed to me I was on target, I was still slightly off. I had missed the mark.

Paul warned the believers in 2 Corinthians 11:1–13 that they need to be careful. It seems there were some people who were claiming to be apostles, but they were just masquerading as apostles. Their teaching might have sounded good, but it was slightly off the mark. They were deceiving people with their false teaching. But then again, Paul wasn't surprised. He reminded the people that even Satan masquerades as an angel of light for he is the great deceiver. He did it in the garden and he is still doing it today. He makes things look so good and sound so right, and yet they are so wrong. Look at how he has even deluded some churches today. On the outside it looks like a church with good social programs or worthy goals, but it does not teach the gospel of Christ or hold to the authority of the Word. It's almost like me shooting at ducks—it looks like I am aiming my shotgun well, and I even shoot at the duck. But I miss the duck…and the mark. Jesus dealt with false teachers in His day, and it is still evident today. Satan did not go away, and he has not changed. He is not done trying to keep people from a true walk of faith in Christ.

There was another time; we were back out on the river. It was fall time—it was duck-hunting time again. The whole family was in the boat and two of my grandsons were out in front of the boat. The result was like the other trips—ducks were being harvested by the boys without much trouble. But as time passed, you guessed it, they talked me into being one of the gunners. Sure enough, after a while I got a shot at a duck. Immediately, the duck folded and fell to the water. We retrieved it and the grandsons examined it. After looking it over thoroughly they looked at me in surprise. There was only one pellet in the duck. It had been hit right in the neck by that one pellet—I had finally hit the mark.

There was no way I was going to let this opportunity pass. I put on a serious face and proceeded to tell the boys that anybody can hit a duck. There are so many pellets going out there when you shoot that you are bound to hit something. It's not like a rifle, where you only have one bullet going out to the target. With the shotgun you have over a hundred pellets going to the target. I continued my teaching moment and informed them that when you get good, you aim in such a way that you only hit the neck. If you can do that, then you won't ruin any of the meat. They looked at me intently, listening to every word. I set the hook well, but after my explanation it only took about two seconds for reality to set in—they then knew I had just fed them a big line. However, it was fun to try to make them think I had a good point.

Paul had a good point when he reminded Timothy to be on guard because there would be false teachers (2 Timothy 4:3–5). These people would conform to the world and say whatever the people wanted to hear.

Again it would be under the guise of Christianity, but it would not line up with Scripture. Therefore, Paul exhorted Timothy to preach the Word—be ready to correct false doctrine and to rebuke the error of the teaching and the teachers. But at the same time, encourage the believers who are walking with the Lord and are following the teachings of God's Word.

I face the same challenge in my own life. It is so easy to be swayed by the world and its teachings. Perhaps not just swayed, but even to the point of accepting that teaching and conforming our life to it. Is that the reason why sometimes it is hard to distinguish the Christian from the non--Christian? Both seem to be thinking and doing the same things. If that is the case, then we have missed the mark of being a true disciple of Christ. We need to become like Timothy and stand firm in our faith. We need to proclaim and follow Scripture. If this would be our testimony, then we would be right on the mark with what God desires.

GONE FISHING

There was steady, sometimes heavy, rain coming down. A flash flood warning had been issued—and sure enough, the little creek behind our house started to get more water than the banks could hold. In short order our house was completely surrounded by water. My grandpa had come over to help my parents move all the furniture from the first floor up to the second floor of the house, hoping to keep it dry. Next, they started to pull up the corner of the carpet in the living room. Then they drilled a hole through the floor so they could watch exactly how close the water was to coming into the house. Meanwhile, as they were busy doing all of this, I stood on the front porch. Amazed at all the water, I thought, *How cool is this! I don't even have to go anywhere to fish—the fish are now right at my doorstep.* So with rod and reel in hand, I began fishing off the porch. At the time, I was just a young boy, but the love for fishing was already there.

There were many years and many miles from the time I stood on that porch back in Ohio until the time I stood on the riverbank in a small village in Alaska. The one thing that stayed consistent throughout the years was a love for fishing. Instead of fishing for catfish or carp, it was now for pike, trout, salmon, and sheefish. One day we made plans for another fishing adventure with our family—but perhaps this adventure would be a little more than fishing from a front porch.

At the time we just had a little twenty-foot johnboat, with a four-foot bottom and a forty-horsepower outboard on the back. It's top speed was twenty-two miles an hour. My old neighbor used to tell me a story about when he was a kid. He was looking at a Sears catalog and saw a ten-horsepower outboard motor for sale and thought how good it would be on the back of a boat. However, his mom said it was way too big of a motor and he would likely get killed having something so big on a boat. He never got to order that outboard. It's funny how times have changed. I was glad I had that forty-horsepower outboard on my boat, even though it was small compared to many of my neighbor's outboard motors.

My family helped load the boat with all the supplies we needed for our fishing trip. The plan was to take the whole day and head up a small river to try pike fishing. We were going about sixty miles upriver to where two forks of the river came together—it seemed like that was always a good place for big pike. Since it was toward the middle of summer, the water level would be a little lower, which would make for better fishing. Slowly, we made our way up the winding little river and after three hours we reached our destination. Now the fishing could begin, and everyone was excited to try to catch a big one.

While we started trying to catch pike, the mosquitoes were trying to catch us—and they were winning! One by one my family started to leave their fishing poles and head into the little wood cabin on the boat. The mosquitoes were horrendous; however, the fishing was good and I just couldn't give it up. So putting on even more bug spray, I continued casting out a lure to try to land another fish. In short order, since the fishing was so good, there were getting to be quite a few pikes lying on the bottom of the boat. Many of these pikes were over forty inches so they were taking up a lot of room.

Casting out along the edge of the bank and reeling in the lure, there was suddenly a distinct hit on the line. This fish seemed like it could be another big one. It was getting complicated trying to work in this fish while also dealing with all the fish on the boat floor. Finally, I pushed some of the fish out of the way to make room. I began pushing one of the bigger pike aside with my boot, but accidentally pushed my boot right into the mouth of the pike. Pikes have big mouths and their teeth point backward, and with my boot firmly lodged into the pike's mouth there was no easy way to flick it off my boot. So with one big pike attached to my right boot I continued to try to move around in the boat and bring in the other pike on my line.

My family, sitting comfortably in the boat cabin, was totally amused with my dilemma. Did they offer to help? Not a chance! Fish on the boot, fish on the line, and swatting at mosquitoes—this was a scene they were enjoying. After a small battle I managed to bring the pike on the line into the boat, and it was another big one. Once that pike was unhooked I then proceeded to try to unhook myself from the pike on my boot. Using two sets of pliers I was able to pry the pike's mouth apart enough that I could pull my boot back out of it. I vividly understood just how effective it was for the pike, having those teeth in its mouth pointing backward. Nothing gets away once the pike latches onto it. It was an amusing fishing adventure, even if I'm not the greatest fisherman.

Interestingly, when Jesus began His ministry the first disciples He called were fishermen. But they didn't fish a river. They fished a lake and probably had some great fish stories to tell. Scripture tells us that there were nights so frustrating for them as they worked hard and didn't catch anything. In any event, they made their living as fishermen. Jesus came along one day and told them to follow Him, and instead of catching fish they would now be fishers of men (Matthew 4:18–19). These men didn't hesitate in their response: they left their nets and followed Christ (Matthew 4:20–22).

These fishermen walked with Jesus for about three years. They were there when Jesus taught from a hillside and in the temple. They were there when Jesus healed a blind man and a sick woman. They were there when he raised up a sick girl from the dead and called Lazarus out from the grave. These men were there at the Last Supper with Jesus before He went to the cross. And they stood at the foot of the cross and witnessed the death and burial of Jesus.

These fishers of men were out fishing in a boat when Jesus appeared to them on the lakeshore. They had a meal with Jesus and then he spent some time talking with Peter (John 21:1–25). This was now the third time that Jesus had appeared to His disciples since He had risen from the dead. Jesus reassured them that the Father would send them the promised Holy Spirit and they would receive power and be His witnesses to the ends of the earth (Acts 1:7). Then, as the disciples stood together, Jesus ascended up into the clouds and was gone. What Jesus had said in the past and what He asked of them to do was suddenly becoming reality—they were to become fishers of men and they were now responsible to make disciples.

Scripture is clear that we, like the disciples, are to be fishers of men; 2 Corinthians 5:20 says, "We are therefore Christ's ambassadors, as though God were making his appeal through us." The disciples were simple fishermen. Their only training was through time spent with Jesus. We, like the disciples, don't need a college degree or a theological degree in order to be Christ's ambassadors. At one time each of us heard the gospel and responded in faith to confess Jesus as our personal Lord and Savior. The issue is being obedient to Scripture and to be His ambassadors.

Looking back at that day on the river catching those big pike, I realized that nothing was going to stop me from fishing. It didn't matter how bad the mosquitoes were or if a fish was stuck on my boot—I was going to keep fishing. The disciples didn't let anything keep them from following the Lord's command to make disciples. It didn't matter if they were beaten or if they were in prison. Whatever the circumstance, they would be faithful to the command to make disciples. What about us? Are we being faithful to the command to make disciples? I need to pray and ask God to help me have the same commitment in making disciples as I did when I was fishing. I need to ask God to help me have the same commitment in making disciples as the ones whom Jesus handpicked two thousand years ago. What about you?

GOOD INTENTIONS

When we were in the village during the early years of ministry, we would only come out of the village once a year. Normally, that would be during the summer since the kids would be out of school. We would take two to three weeks out of the village and divide our time between the mission's conference and our mini-vacation. Everyone was always excited for this time. Since this was such a special time, I had good intentions of making the time out of the village memorable.

This was a time to reengage with our Western white culture. After spending fifty weeks in the native setting, this brought us back to our roots. With the village being two hundred and fifty miles from the road system, this was also a time to do all the things found in the city—such as just taking a ride, getting some ice cream, and eating at fast-food restaurants. We were all like kids in a candy store when we would first get to the city. We wanted to try everything we had missed over the last year.

One summer we had a special opportunity offered by one of the mission families. They were going to be out of town the same time we were going to be in town. They asked us to housesit for them while they were gone. This was a huge blessing for our family. We had the chance to play basketball, mow a lawn, and have more room in a house than we knew what to do with. While we were there the weather was perfect. Everyone pitched in to help do whatever chores needed to be done; however, there was one job that only I could do.

It is always interesting when you get to housesit for someone. You can find out what things they really like. Do they have a big lawn? Do they have a big grill out back? What kind of special items do they have in the house? Do they have a pool table or ping-pong table? Our friend's house had a lot of plants. We were given instructions on how to keep them alive. Obviously, this was of utmost importance and I had good intentions to do the job right. There was one special plant that only I would be able to take care of, and it hung high up in the entry foyer of the house

Everyone helped, and in short order all the plants were watered—now onto the special plant. The plants were scattered throughout the house, but I couldn't quite understand the location of this one special plant. Why would anyone put a plant in a location where you would have to bring a stepladder into the house to water it? Well, my job was not to question why, but to simply make sure it got watered. The last thing I wanted was to kill this plant since the family was nice enough to let us stay in their house. So I brought the stepladder from the garage and set it up in the entryway under the plant. Good thing it was an eight-foot stepladder because that plant was high up. I carefully climbed the ladder, had my wife hand me a container of water, and slowly began watering the plant. I wasn't sure how much water to add, but I didn't have to worry. Shortly after dispensing some of the water into the plant pot, it began to flow out the bottom. I was shocked at first, then immediately stopped pouring any more water. Sure enough, after some careful inspection, the artificial plant didn't need much water. I climbed back down, put the ladder away and proceeded to mop the floor.

Could it be possible that for a second year we would be blessed with another house-sitting opportunity? This family was off to do their summer fishing at a village along the Aleutian chain. We were given a chance to stay at their house during the time we would be out of the village. The house was amazing and my wife and I had a bedroom with more than just one quarter of an inch of plywood dividing us from the kids. Not only did we have real walls, but the kids didn't have to walk through our bedroom to get out of their bedroom. We were so blessed! One more thing: the master bedroom had its own bathroom. But this was not an ordinary bathroom—this bathroom had a Jacuzzi.

It was an amazing two weeks staying at this house. Our family had the opportunity to do so many exciting things, like playing basketball, jumping on a trampoline, playing crochet, and running all over the yard. While we were staying at the house, I decided my wife and I should have a special time in the Jacuzzi. I knew that this would require an awful lot of hot water, but I thought maybe one time would be okay. One thing I knew for sure—we were not going to have an opportunity like this for a long time.

The kids had gone to bed and so we proceeded to the master bedroom. I went into the bathroom and began to run the water. I wanted this time to be special for my wife. She'd dealt with many difficult things in the village, so this was going to be a great time for her to relax. It would be a time to leave the rest of the world behind, at least for a little while, and let that water soak in and relax her muscles. Perhaps this would take away some of the stress and tension she sometimes felt. The water was slowly filling up in the tub, and as I began to look around in the bathroom I spotted something that might help make this evening even a little better.

There on the shelf was a bottle of bubble bath. Now I don't know much about these things, but I had heard that women sometimes liked bubble bath. I took the bottle, unscrewed the lid, and poured some of the liquid into the water. After a time, the water had almost reached the height it needed to be and I looked once more at that bottle of bubble bath. It might be a good idea to add a little more, so I poured more of this special liquid into the water—this was going to be a great experience for my wife.

We climbed into the Jacuzzi and then I turned on that magical switch, the one that starts making the water jettison all around in the tub. Did I know exactly how bubble bath worked? No. However, it became rapidly apparent to me. Bubbles began rising at an alarming rate and overflowing the tub. We began to try to swat the bubbles down to break them, but it was futile. The bubbles came faster than we could knock them down. They quickly reached a height to where they were going to cover our faces. Frantically, I remembered where the magical switch was and reached through all the bubbles to turn it off.

I found out soon enough that a little bubble bath goes a long way. We cleared all the bubbles out of the Jacuzzi and decided to try it again. I reached around, turned the switch on, and watched in amazement as the bubbles once again returned. Seemingly undeterred, the bubbles again proceeded to grow to the point of covering our faces. I turned the switch off again and knew I had met our match. The bubble bath won. It truly was a good idea and I had good intentions, but without a doubt I had added too much bubble bath.

Likewise, Peter had good intentions. They had arrested Jesus and took him away, so Peter followed behind and made it to the courtyard. At least he had come—he had told Jesus that he would not fall away and he would even lay his own life down if needed. Peter had good intentions that evening he arrived at the courtyard (John 13:37–38). It was dark, and he was outnumbered. The crowd was set against Jesus and it appeared Peter was alone. Then came the question. "You aren't one of this man's disciples, too, are you?" (John 18:17). Peter, with all his good intentions, fell back and denied he even knew Jesus. The first of three denials just transpired.

Sometimes we are quick to point our finger at Peter and wonder how he could have done such a thing. But are we really any different? We, too, have God's Word, His Spirit lives in us, and we have good intentions to follow Him; 1 Peter 1:14–15 reminds us not to follow our old evil desires, but rather to be holy as He is holy. And Romans 12:2 teaches us to not conform any longer to this world, but to change and be like Him. How are we doing? Do our good intentions sometimes fall short? Do we fail to walk with Him and follow Him completely? Are we any different than Peter? Perhaps we, like Peter, need to fall on our face and repent before our Lord. Then we must finish our life as Peter did—one where good intentions eventually led to obedience and faith.

How Deep the
Father's Love

Hebrews 2:6 says, "What is man that you are mindful of them?" As I get older, I am more and more amazed at the grace the Lord has shown me. It brings to my mind the words of the song "How Deep the Father's Love for Us" by Stuart Townend.

One of the important times of the year is when hunting season begins. It is more than just a sport. It is a means of putting food on the table for the year. The largest animal we hunt in bush Alaska is the moose. Standing about seven feet at the shoulder and weighing three quarters of a ton, there is a healthy supply of meat on the hoof. Some seasons hunting becomes a little more challenging in finding a good bull.

One fall we were working hard to find a bull. We had spent a good part of the time on the river and checking meadows, but to no avail. I decided to try a different area, accessible only by canoe. I was sure no one else was in this area. The morning my son and I headed out the air was chilly—there was frost on everything and no wind. The season was getting far enough along that the rut was getting stronger, which would help in our effort to locate a moose.

We carried the canoe down to the lake and the plan was to paddle across it, portage the canoe for half a mile, and then put in on a small slough. There had always been moose in this area in the past, and we were hopeful as we set out. With my son in the front, we paddled across the lake. The exercise of paddling felt good and warmed me up in the chilly air. Since it was early in the morning and there was no wind, the lake was perfectly calm and not a sound was heard. With the start of the day, light was just beginning to show, which made for a peaceful setting. We made our way toward the other side of the lake and began working our way through some little fingers of water—the tough portage was about to begin.

We dug our paddles into the water and worked them to maneuver the canoe around the final twists and turns. Finally, our paddles hit the bottom of the lake as the point of the canoe struck the shore. I steadied the canoe while my son stepped onto the bank and he began to pull the canoe up onto the bank. I decided to get out of the canoe to give him a hand in dragging the canoe the rest of the way up the bank, but when I took a couple of steps forward I suddenly found a deep hole. I went down to my waist in the frigid water before I could step back onto shallower water. I stood wet and cold in disbelief. How could it be so deep when all around it was shallow? I was only standing a couple feet from dry ground, but apparently that was a couple feet too far. The temperature was below freezing and I needed to get dry and warm quickly. We got back in the canoe and headed for home.

It felt great to get back home and find some dry clothes, and stand by the woodstove to warm up. I never would have imagined how deep that hole on the edge of the lake could have been. This, however, was not my last experience with deep water.

One of my favorite times of flying is in the summer. When that season comes it means that the wheels are taken off the plane and the floats are installed. Float flying brings a smile to my face. Gliding on the water during takeoff, landings with unlimited water runways, being able to land and takeoff into the wind, and fishing from the floats always makes for an adventure. But float flying does come with some challenges. One such incident occurred in a village upriver.

It was the time of year when I fly for Bible camp. Bringing kids to and from camp kept my days full. I flew kids from different villages to the camp for a week of Bible teaching along with games and fun activities. The kids always looked forward to camp time.

I flew into camp one day to pick up another load of kids to bring them back home. It was always interesting to take the kids to camp because it seemed someone would always get airsick. On the way home, it was a different story. Most of the kids were so tired they would sleep during the entire flight—hardly did anyone get airsick on the way back to their village. I loaded three kids into the plane with their gear and headed to their home village. After a one-hour flight, I began circling over the village and noticed my normal landing site on the river was not available. Someone in the village had set nets out, trying to catch the salmon that were migrating upstream. Since the nets were in the water, it also meant that some of the boats had been repositioned.

I surveyed the river and knew I would have to land a little farther upriver than normal. That usually wasn't a problem; however, this would prove interesting today. I knew that as you went upriver there was the start of a sandbar and the water started getting shallow. Yet there would be no choice—I would have to land farther up the river. After touching down on the water, I began to taxi toward the bank. I felt the drag on the floats as they touched bottom. Unfortunately, it was way short of the bank. What I suspected might happen became reality. I wore waders for such a time as this. I stepped onto the float and then into the water and began pushing the plane free from the bottom of the river. As the plane began to break free I realized that the current might rotate my plane around. The back end of the plane could be carried by the current and turned into the bank, right where the boats were parked.

Sure enough, the back end swung around toward the boats. I didn't want to damage anyone's boat and I certainly didn't want to damage my floats by hitting a boat, so I quickly climbed up on the float and headed to the back of it. Fortunately, I wasn't too far from the bank and it looked like I might miss the boats. I knew I better get the plane to the riverbank, so I grabbed one of the float tie-down ropes and gracefully stepped off the back of the float and into the water. Hip waders are called hip waders for a reason. They do an incredible job of keeping you dry—that is, if the water isn't over your hip! The bank gave no indication of the water's depth, and as I stepped into the water it became obvious that this water was deep—deeper than the top of my waders. All I could do at this point was keep heading for the bank. Though I was soaked, at least I had saved my plane from hitting any of the boats.

I tied the plane to the bank and began unloading the kids and their gear. After I had finished, I decided it was time to empty out my hip waders. As I pulled them off and dumped all the water out, a lady on the bank made a profound statement. "Well, at least you know they don't leak." I had to laugh, thinking there are probably better ways than stepping into deep water to find this out.

The water in both situations was deeper than I thought—it was hard to imagine how deep that water could have been. Likewise, it is hard to envision how deep the Father's love is for us. Jesus says in John 10:18 that the Father had given His Son the command to lay down His life. I am a sinner and although I continue to sin, the Father's love is so deep that He sent His Son to die for me. How am I to imagine this depth of love? Do I totally understand it? No. I am grateful the Father sat on His thrown in heaven, watching as His Son went to the cross, for me. That is love beyond words and beyond comprehension. It's a Father's deep love.

How Strong is My Faith?

We were making our way up a small river for a family outing—a little fishing and a picnic to enjoy the day. Along the way we did our usual stop for a break. I walked back into the woods to have a look around. Then I spotted it—a moose carcass. The rack made it obvious that it was a bull. The difference with this one was that it had some dirt and a little brush piled on it. I began to look around, oblivious to the fact that this was a grizzly cache and unaware of the potential danger that it held. Did I understand that the bear would defend his food cache? Not likely. This was our first summer in Alaska. Fortunately for me, nothing happened and I headed back to the boat. No doubt I was new to the country, but I hoped to live long enough to learn about the land.

Later, I learned what I should have known then: this was a different land than any other place I had lived. This was a land that held potential danger. I began to understand why you pack a rifle with you whenever you venture out into this land. Through the years I have also learned that you need to be careful, and not just only for bears. If you make a mistake, there's no 9-1-1 to call—a mistake could end up costing you your life. This is an unforgiving land. Unfortunately, there are times when people make a mistake and pay a price. That scenario happens too often. Through the years my knowledge and experience of this place called Alaska grew. Down the trail of life, I had a couple of other experiences with grizzly bears, but one I remember quite vividly.

Every year we would begin the fall-harvesting process. My wife enjoyed getting out and gathering all the different berries—cranberries, salmon berries, raspberries, and blueberries. The freezer full of berries meant it was time to harvest some meat. There might be a chance of harvesting a caribou in the spring, but that was dependent upon their migration route. The surest supply of meat would be the moose. But every time we went hunting, we were not the only ones hunting moose. There were always the wolves on the prowl, and also the grizzly bear.

One fall, as we were heading upriver to set up a hunting camp, my son-in-law and I noticed a group of ravens along the riverbank in the early light. We decided to check it out on our return trip to the village. Ravens were always worth watching. They could give clues as to what was happening in the area. With our supplies off-loaded at camp, we turned the boat back downriver. As we approached the area we wanted to search, we realized no intense searching was necessary. As the ravens flew away, there on the bank lay a dead cow moose. Looking at the sign it was obvious this was a grizzly kill. We could tell that it was fresh and that the bear was probably just lying back in the brush. This would be worth our effort—perhaps we could hunt this grizzly.

Later that day we moved the rest of the supplies plus all the family up to the hunting camp. Though our priority would be moose, we had not forgotten what lay downriver. We came up with a plan, hoping to try the next evening. As we looked for moose the next morning we came up empty. However, we enjoyed the day on the river, seeing the autumn colors and enjoying the quiet and solitude. That evening, as the others sat around the campfire, my son-in-law and I prepared to head downriver. Just as we were ready to leave, a boat came upriver and stopped at our camp. They informed us they had seen a grizzly bear on a moose carcass. As they had come closer, the bear took off back into the brush. We decided that our chance for this day was done.

We woke the next morning as the quiet was interrupted by some ducks going by on the river. The stars were giving way to dawn—another good day to be out in the woods. With nothing happening during the day with the moose, our thoughts again turned downriver. We decided we would try the same approach we had planned that previous night. We got into the boat and headed down the river. Once we were half a mile above the kill area, we turned off the motor and began to drift. Looking through binoculars we could see the bear on the bank, by his moose, so we slowly drifted downriver to give us time to watch the bear.

The strength of a grizzly bear is something to marvel. As we watched, the bear decided to try to hide the carcass. He grabbed the moose and began to drag it up the steep bank. This bank is something that would prove a challenge for me just to climb up it. But the bear dragged the carcass of about 600 pounds up the bank. After getting halfway up the bank, the carcass got stuck and he couldn't get it any higher. And back down the bank went the carcass as the frustrated bear took it back to the original starting place. During this whole time, we were getting closer with each passing second—and soon we didn't need binoculars to see the bear.

In the quiet of the evening, as we approached closer, we could hear the bear chewing on the carcass; we heard bones cracking. In the evening light, as we drifted closer, we saw the bear clearly in our open sights. We drifted to less than a 100 yards from the bear because we wanted to get as close as possible. Then we began to fire. Instinctively, the bear began running up the steep bank. We could tell that he was hit and he turned, not being able to climb up the bank. Flames flew from the end of the barrels as the bullets were launched on their way—with some connecting and others entering the mud. With the animal on the move not every shot was hitting the intended target. At this juncture my son-in-law needed to reload, and I had one left in the chamber.

We drifted down the river to the point where we were directly across from the bear. He looked in our direction, jumped into the river, and started coming right at us. I fired my final round, but it didn't stop him. My son-in-law quickly loaded one round directly into the chamber and fired at pointblank range as the bear closed in on the boat. The hunt was ended. As we prepared to take care of the bear, we realized how heavy the animal was. The adrenaline began to subside, but there was more than just adrenaline coursing through our bodies. I realized that there was a certain amount of fear as the bear had charged directly at us. I could only imagine what that bear could do to a person. I know the length of the front claws, the power in his arms, and the strength of his jaws—yes, our fear was solidly based.

Look at the account in Daniel. He either heard about or saw the fear people felt when they were thrown into the lion's den. He possibly heard the stories of the lion's strength in tearing apart humans who were cast into the pit. He knew this fear was based upon reality. This would all come into play in Daniel's life in an unusual way. Daniel chapter 6 gives us the details.

There was jealousy within the leadership of the kingdom—nothing unusual. The 120 satraps along with two of the administrators were upset with Daniel. The king, being deceived by these leaders, set up a new law: no prayer the next month except to the king, and failure to comply with this law would mean being put in the lion's pit. These leaders conceived what they thought was a flawless plan to get rid of Daniel. They knew Daniel would still pray to his God and death would be imminent for him.

Again, Daniel knew all too well about the lion's den. He was now aware of the new law. But fear did not grip Daniel. Daniel felt no fear, even if he faced the lions with nothing to protect himself. Yet I felt fear facing a bear even though I had a gun. Daniel knew he had the Lord. He went to his room and prayed three times a day, just as was normal. Sure enough, the king was made aware of the fact that Daniel was violating the new law. With disappointment and concern the king sent Daniel to the lion's den. Daniel had faith. Faith he could put complete trust in his God, no matter the circumstance or the outcome. A faith that overcame fear. The next day, when the king came to the pit, he was surprised that Daniel was still alive. But Daniel was not surprised. His faith was rewarded. He was alive. This makes me wonder, *How strong is my faith? Do I let the circumstances dictate my faith? Do I completely trust the Lord regardless of the outcome?* I need to have faith—a faith that will even overcome fear.

IT MUST BE OKAY

Everything was perfect—and it was so. God walked with Adam and Eve in the garden and He provided everything they needed. Only one thing was off-limits—only one restriction: do not eat the fruit of this one tree. Apparently, it seems that Satan does not need much of an opening to tempt us to fall. According to the account given in Genesis 3, Satan was successful—man fell. Satan called the Word of God into question and he twisted what God had said. He made it all seem good, right, and okay.

Hunting season was over, and the meat all put away—winter was on its way. This was always an interesting time of the year, a time of transition. The liquid water turned solid. The water highway was no longer available for boat travel. Not only was the river freezing but all the lakes and sloughs. It's always a good thing when the snow doesn't come right away as this gives all the waterways a chance to freeze solid and make transportation by snowmobile much safer once the snow comes.

This year the start to winter was a good one. Everything was freezing and the snow was absent, making for thicker ice. Kids were already playing and skating on the lake by the village, although travel was restricted with the lack of snow—this being one of the main drawbacks, but one could still manage to get around in the village via leg power. However, for one family this situation raised a new challenge.

Roughly forty miles to the northwest of the village lived a family at the foot of the mountains—homesteaders. They were related to the village people and so there was always a concern for how the family was doing. During the summer we would see them on the river, and during the winter, once the snow came, they would visit the village by snowmobile. This year, with no snow, contact with them was now impossible—that is, until I had purchased a small two-seat airplane.

The village council approached me to see if there were any possibilities I could fly out to their cabin, circle over them, and see if they were all right. *Let the adventure begin,* I thought. The airplane was just a fabric airplane with only an eighty-five-horsepower engine—not a great performer, but something affordable. I got the airplane ready for the flight. I put fuel on board, did the preflight check, and gave a rough timeframe for my flight to the village people. Since there was an open spot beside me on the sling seat, I decided to ask my elder neighbor if he wanted to come with me. He was glad to go and get a great chance to see the countryside as well as check on the family.

It was cold outside as we headed for the little airplane. I already knew from experience that the small knob for heat wouldn't really make a difference with these cold temperatures. Rather, I bundled up well enough to try to stay warm. My neighbor climbed into the plane while I prepared it for start-up—slightly crack the throttle, set the brakes, turn on the switch, and go to the front of the plane. Hand propping an airplane since there were no electrics was always exciting. After a few flips of the prop the engine came to life. I climbed in, fastened my seatbelt, and prepared for departure.

As I taxied toward the runway, people watched our departure. I knew they would be back at the airport when we returned, especially since the airport was close by the village. It is always exciting to lift off the runway, begin to climb, and watch the world unfold below you. Suddenly, you have a whole new perspective of the land beneath you—you can see the animal trails, the winding of the waterways, and the land that lies far off in the distance. Immediately after liftoff we could see the mountains that this family called home. We set our course in their direction and began enjoying the flight.

Within half an hour we were circling over the cabin and watching the family exiting their home to eagerly wave to the occupants of the little grey airplane above them. After we had made several flybys and knew that the family was safe, we decided to head back to the village. The mission was accomplished and the villagers would hear our report and be relieved, knowing the family was okay.

Once we turned back for the village, there was a common sensation that came over me—I needed to go to the bathroom. Unfortunately, this was not a commercial jet airliner and there were no bathrooms located in the back. I began to consider my options. Some of them didn't seem too appealing. Then it came to me: the lakes were frozen, so I would land on a lake to relieve myself. I knew the lake by the village was frozen solid and I assumed the lakes that I was flying over would be the same. Having lived in the village a while, I knew the best thing to do was ask the elder sitting beside me what he thought.

I looked at the elder beside me and asked, "Do you think it's okay to land on this lake?"

He looked at me and said one word. "Yah."

That was all I needed to hear. Before time ran out and other undesirable options became reality I circled the lake to set up an approach for the landing spot I had chosen. When it is cold, the performance of an airplane is much better since the air is denser. The landing approach was looking good and as I came close to the lake I slowed the plane down, working to get a smooth landing. As soon as my wheels hit the ice the whole situation dramatically changed.

The ice began to crack and sink under the weight of the airplane, and water began to rush to the surface. Immediately the prop wash picked up the water and began to spray it onto the plane. As the ice cracked, I pushed the throttle full forward. How I wished I had a little more horsepower! The elder who had said only one word up to this point now became vocal. I wasn't sure what he was saying and didn't want to dialogue at this point.

The airplane slowly picked up speed and miraculously stayed on top of the ice, which continued to break underneath us. It seemed like a long time before I had enough speed to get the plane airborne. With a huge sigh of relieve, I turned the airplane back in the direction of the village. As I looked out the window I could see that the water had already frozen and ice was hanging onto parts of the airplane.

Soon we were back over the village and coming in for a landing. Just as expected, the people were there on the ramp, waiting to get our report on the family. As I taxied up to the parking spot, I could see the people looking intently at the airplane. As we climbed out of the plane, the people came up and asked what had happened. I proceeded to tell them how I wanted to land on a lake and had asked the elder if it was okay, to which he had said "yah." His wife, who was listening to the report, walked right up to him and said with a pointed finger, "How many times have I told you? If you can't hear what they are saying, then quit saying, 'Yah.'"

Although the ice appeared safe it was a death trap. Paul wrote in Ephesians 6:10–12 that Satan is our real enemy and he will do whatever he can to make us fall. He will do whatever he can to lead us into a death trap. We are in a very real spiritual battle every day. Satan loves to see each of us fail in our spiritual walk. When he tempts us he makes the situation appear okay. He distorts God's Word and messes with our thinking. The outcome of following his temptation can have deadly results. It is no different today than it was back in the days of Adam and Eve. We all need to be careful in what we say "yah" to and remember to fight off the temptation of Satan.

Learning

to Trust God

"**M**ayday! Mayday!" This was the distress call I gave over the airplane radio late one spring morning. The preflight, run-up, and takeoff were uneventful. However, shortly into the flight the engine had a major malfunction—a rod came out through the engine case. Oil was spewing out of the engine, and as a result black smoke poured out from the cowling. In the subsequent crash, the airplane had been destroyed. "What would be the future of my flying?" That was the question I now asked myself. Without an airplane much of my ministry would come to an end.

Arriving home after the crash, my wife and I began to discuss how flying would fit into our future ministry. I felt it was important for the flying ministry to continue; however, we didn't have any insurance on the airplane. Not only did we have no insurance, but we didn't have any funds that could help replace the airplane. This was one of the times in my life when I questioned God as to why He had allowed this to happen.

First things first—if the flying ministry is to continue, what airplane would I need? A Cessna 180 would be a good airplane for our present ministry situation, but I was aware of what this airplane would cost. My wife questioned me regarding what I felt I really needed in an airplane. "I just want to fly," I replied, and a Cessna 180 was my first choice.

Then she said, "Let's pray and see what God will do."

Where will the funds come from for this airplane? Well, the mission organization we were with offered to help us raise funds to purchase an airplane. They agreed to send out a letter to their mailing list, explaining what had happened and the need for another airplane. This was good news; however, this would be a large financial undertaking. The letters were sent and now it was time to wait and pray. The office informed me that I would be able to call in and they would keep me updated on any financial response to the letter.

We had been in the village four years and it was time to go visit some of our supporters in the lower forty-eight. The timing would be good. We would visit our supporters during the summer months, when the kids were out of school and while we were without the airplane. Visiting supporters is always an encouraging time, yet tiring and potentially stressful. But reconnecting with the part of the team that supports you in prayer and finances is also rewarding and important. As we were traveling through the states once in a while, I would contact the mission office to see if any funds for the airplane had come in.

The report was encouraging. Money was starting to come in to fund another airplane. As the lazy days of summer passed by, we continued visiting our supporting churches. But my mind would always drift back to the airplane need. We were not sure what kind of response this need would generate from the letters the mission sent. Toward the end of the summer, the mission organization informed me that monies were coming in at a higher rate for this project than they had ever experienced before on any other project. We were excited to hear this news! Now we just had to wait for a grand total.

With the end of summer we returned to the village. I began to check the various sources that listed airplanes for sale, looking for a Cessna 180 that had the equipment that would meet my flying needs. Through the first couple weeks as I searched ads, none of the airplanes seemed to be what I needed. A final call was made to the mission office and they gave me the total figure of the monies raised for the airplane. The amount was unbelievable! People had responded in an amazing way and God had been faithful. Now I just needed to be patient and wait for the right airplane.

September came, and I made my way down to the field office for a meeting. At the end of the meeting, before I headed home, I decided to look at the local paper to see if there were any planes for sale. Sure enough, there was a Cessna 180 that had just been listed. I called on the airplane and then contacted another mission organization in the area that worked on airplanes. Arrangements were made to meet with one of their mechanics and go look at the airplane. Upon inspection of the plane, everything seemed in order and the airplane had some valuable extras that would come with it. Included with the sale would be hydraulic wheel skis for winter use and a set of floats for the summer. This would be perfect!

Now it came down to the money. Contacting the mission home office one final time, they informed me that I would have to pay taxes on the money that had been received for my airplane. The amount set aside for taxes would be $12,000.00. The owner selling the airplane wanted $68,000.00. Between taxes and the airplane, that would bring the total to $80,000.00 needed to complete the deal. I asked the mission organization how much money had come in, and their response was $80,000.00. Not a penny less and not a penny more—exactly what I needed.

Late September found me flying the newly purchased Cessna 180 back to my home village. Visiting with my wife over the phone, I indicated to her that this would be a good airplane for ministry—the only negative in my mind was the color. The plane was predominantly yellow. I don't really like yellow. Knowing this, my wife informed the kids that when I landed in the village they were not to say anything about the color of the airplane. Apparently, that information didn't get passed onto the neighbor boy who spent a lot of time at our house. When the family greeted me at the village gravel strip, the first words out of the neighbor boy's mouth was, "That sure is an ugly color." I had to agree with him. However, the one positive thing about a yellow airplane is the color shows up clearly in the sky.

In less than six months, when all had seemed hopeless after losing my airplane, God provided a plane for my ministry. When it was obvious that we had no means within ourselves to get another airplane, God was faithful to supply one. Looking at the airplane sitting on the ramp, I stood amazed at what had transpired through the summer—a plane that far surpassed my old one had been provided by God in a miraculous way. Slowly, God was teaching me to trust in Him.

I remember a great account found in Scripture where trust in the Lord had been displayed. The account is found in Exodus. After years of slavery, God's people, the Israelites, were about to be set free from bondage. Moses was called by God to lead His people to the Promised Land. In Exodus 12, the pharaoh told Moses to take his people and leave. About 600,000 men, plus women and children, were now led by Moses and leaving Egypt behind. However, they did not travel far before they were confronted with a dire situation.

Exodus 14:5–9 records how once the Israelites left Egypt, the pharaoh changed his mind. He decided he had made a mistake and therefore gathered his army and went after Moses and the Israelites. When the Israelites saw the army of the pharaoh approaching, they were terrified. It is hard to comprehend what that army must have been like, considering the number of Israelite men. Yet the pharaoh's army looked so intimidating that all the Israelites turned to Moses in fear for their lives. Undaunted, Moses stood before the people and reassured them that the Lord would deliver His people that day (Exodus 14:13–14).

How strong was the trust that Moses must have had in the Lord! Strong enough that he could stand with his people, with the Red Sea on one side and the Egyptian army on the other side, and told them not to fear. God would fight for you. He would deliver you today. Trust your God. Exodus 14:15–30 describes how God parted the water, letting the Israelites cross on dry ground. Then the pharaoh and his army pursued the Israelites, marching onto the dry seabed between the walls of water, confident of their upcoming victory. Suddenly, the water let loose and the pharaoh and all his men were killed as the water crashed upon them. The Israelites stood on the far shore, watching as the Lord eliminated their enemy. "And when the Israelites saw the mighty hand of the Lord displayed against the Egyptians, the people feared the Lord and put their trust in Him and in Moses His servant" (Exodus 14:31).

The Lord was working in my life through the airplane experience to help me learn to put my trust in Him. Am I close to the depth of trust that Moses displayed in this account of Scripture? Not even close! However, my prayer is that the Lord will help me grow deeper, day by day, to trust in Him—trusting Him not just in the big things but in everyday matters of life.

Learning to Trust,
Part Two

It was a stormy summer day. Dark clouds were hanging low along the hills with the wind moving them at will. Rain was scattered throughout the landscape—these weren't the best conditions to fly people to another village for ministry. The people had come from the lower forty-eight, to lead a Vacation Bible School (VBS) program for the kids. Everything had been planned: times were set, money was raised, teaching materials had been organized, and travel schedules arranged. But now we all faced the storm. Unlike the lower forty-eight, there were no roads for travel. This trip was all dependent upon the airplane. We only had one hundred and thirty miles ahead of us, but that distance seemed almost insurmountable.

Walking up and down the lake bank, we slowly loaded the float plane with supplies. After stowing most of the supplies in the float lockers, the three passengers climbed aboard. Firing up the engine and taxiing to one end of the lake, I prepared for departure. Seeing the waves on the lake reminded me that the wind would aid in the takeoff run. Slowly the float plane built up speed and lifted off the water. After the departure we began the trip north, looking at the gloomy weather ahead. After a couple of failed attempts of trying to push our way through the storm, I turned the plane back to the south and headed home. It wasn't going to work today—but at least we were alive to try again tomorrow. Tomorrow is another day.

Another time there was an unexpected phone call, but not an unusual one. The individual had left one village, headed for another, but had never showed up. The people calling mentioned that the person should have arrived yesterday. They wondered if I could fly and look for the missing person. Laying everything else aside, I began to get the airplane ready for another search-and-rescue flight. The land up here is unforgiving and one mistake could end up being your last one—there is no 9-1-1 emergency number to call. Everything was ready for the flight, and with no time to spare I departed with a prayer for the mission.

These two separate airplane scenarios are common here. Each flight was different in purpose and focus, but both were part of ministry flying I have done throughout the years. There were other flights for funerals, work teams, visiting villages, or going to encourage other missionaries. Flights were also made across the mountains to attend mission meetings helping to provide leadership. Throughout the years all these flights added hours to the use of the airplane.

Airplanes are no different from other mechanical devices in many ways. Eventually they wear out. Airplane engines have a limit to the number of hours they can be used before the engine must be inspected and rebuilt. My engine in the Cessna 180 had reached that hourly limit. Standing in the mechanic shop in Fairbanks, he presented some options I had for the engine. The two main options were: to rebuild my existing engine or to upgrade to a larger remanufactured engine. After considering the costs, the length of time before another engine overhaul, and the horsepower of the engines, I went with the new and larger engine. With this larger engine would come a three-bladed prop instead of the current two-bladed prop I owned. This prop would also provide better performance—and due to this, it would increase the cost of the project.

My mechanic began explaining to me the process for getting this new engine. The main point he made was that the engine company would require larger payments as they were working through the process. This new setup for the engine and prop was going to cost roughly $40,000.00. "How much money do you have to put toward the new engine?" my mechanic asked.

"Well, not much. Actually, not anything," was my response. "However, I can send a letter to my supporters and let them know of my need and see what happens." With that understanding, I had the mechanic place the engine order and we prayed for the Lord to raise up people who would help us with this project.

Funds began to come in and I was able make the payments to the company and keep the process moving forward. As I continued to fly there were signs confirming that it was definitely time to change out this old engine. Finally, one day as I was in the mechanic's shop, he informed me that the engine company was ready for the final payment. Once this payment was received, they could finish the last details on the engine and send it my way. I asked the mechanic what the final payment was and he let me know it was $12,000.00. He asked me if I had the money and I bluntly told him the truth that I didn't have any of the money needed. "What do you want me to tell the engine manufacturer?" he asked.

I responded, "Tell them to finish the engine and get it ready to send it my way." My mechanic looked at me in surprise and asked how I planned on making that final payment. I told him that I didn't know, but that God did and He would provide, though I didn't know exactly how.

My wife and I left the city and flew home to the village. We had only been at home a couple of days when late one afternoon my wife told me I should read an email that had just come in. I went upstairs, sat down by the computer, and began to read.

"My wife and I would like to help with the airplane engine but don't know where to send the money. Could you give us an address of where to send it? By the way, we will be sending $12,000.00."

God had laid it upon the heart of this old preacher and his wife to help me with the engine and how much to send. I sat there looking at the screen feeling amazed, blessed, humble, and unworthy. God had provided! Shortly thereafter, my airplane was in the shop with a new engine and prop being placed on the frame. Once again, I was learning to trust my God.

Trusting God in providing an airplane engine is one thing, but trusting God when your life is on the line is another. James, the brother of John, had been killed with the sword. Because this pleased the Jews, Herod had Peter also arrested. There would be a trial; however, the church and even Peter must have wondered what the outcome would be. There would probably be another death. Peter would be the martyr—it seemed simple and straightforward because, of course, who could go against King Herod? So Peter was put in prison guarded by four squads of four soldiers each. Not only that, but he was bound with chains behind locked doors. What were Peter and the church to do?

Acts 12:5 says that the church was earnestly praying to God. I can imagine that there were prayers asking the Lord to spare the life of Peter. Certainly, the believers weren't sure how this could happen, with no way of stopping Herod, but by faith they continued to pray. The Feast of Unleavened Bread was soon coming to an end and Herod would be bringing Peter to trial.

Then it happened. Late at night, an angel of the Lord stood before Peter in the jail cell. The angel told Peter to get his clothes on because they were leaving the cell. The chains fell off and they walked past the guards. The city gates opened and the angel left Peter there, alone on the street. Acts 12:12 says that Peter, still trying to figure out what had happened, went to the house of Mary where the believers had gathered to pray. Little did they know that while they were praying, Peter was already free—God had answered their prayer. Peter went to the door and knocked and finally stood inside the house, explaining to the believers everything that had happened. They had prayed, and God had answered. Their trust in God had been strengthened.

And so it is even today—God allows things to come into the early church's lives and into our lives so that we might learn to trust Him.

God allowed my experience with the airplane engine to help in developing my trust in God. It isn't an easy process and it's not that we ever attain to the depth of trust that God desires, but there should be a steady growth of trust as we go through situations like these. Seeing God answer prayers when all seems hopeless and seeing God respond to us in situations where there seems to be no possible solution, all bolster our depth of trust in God. May we be willing to not allow the situation or circumstance to cause us to lose hope. May we learn to stand firm in our trust of the Lord and be willing to share our story and give glory to our God. Let this be our testimony for all the world to see.

Mayday, Mayday!

I was just a kid when I watched my uncle fly a model airplane. The airplane, on the end of a string, went around and around in a circle. Eventually it crashed to the ground. I thought that was pretty cool! That was the beginning of my love for airplanes. Throughout the years, this passion for planes and flying never went away. The opportunity to do something with flying never seemed to become reality—that is, until we were living in Colorado.

Just like my uncle, I began to fly model airplanes. The difference this time was that I wasn't using a string, but a remote control. The greatest joy was to build the airplanes, which came in a kit. Glue all the balsa together and watch it fly. My wife used to think that radio-control flying was a great family sport. While I attempted to fly the plane, much like my uncle's experience, it would end up crashing. Thus, the great family sport turned into all the family members helping to pick up all the little pieces of balsa from the ground. That love of flying turned from radio control to real airplanes as the Lord began to direct our steps toward missionary service.

When I was in my upper thirties, the Lord began to give me a clear call to be a missionary. My wife knew she was called by the Lord to be a missionary when she was a teenager. Finally, our calls were coming together, in His timing, and to the field of His choosing. We both got a call to go and work in Alaska with the native people. Eventually, we would be involved in a church-planting effort in a small village. Part of the ministry would involve the use of an airplane, and so I began to take pilot training. After completing the ground school and the flight training, I received my pilot's license. Flying had moved from a fascination to a reality.

Part of the flight-training program involved emergency procedures. One part of the training involved handling an engine failure. I remember the instructor teaching me a good saying to remember the proper order to follow in an emergency. "If you have a problem," he said, "you may get a little tense and thirsty, so what you need is 'ANRC.'" Back in that day there was a cola drink called RC Cola. A was for aviate—fly the airplane. N was for navigate—figure out where you can land. R was for resuscitate—try and start the engine. C was for communicate—let someone know of your situation. We went over and over that process so that it became a part of me.

After two years of living in the village, I purchased my first airplane. This airplane was a little two-seater. It was slow, but provided a good opportunity to build time and experience. After having that airplane for a couple years, I made the switch to a four-passenger plane. The ministry was expanding and I needed a larger plane to carry more people and freight. I purchased the airplane from a man in the lower forty-eight, and so I went out there to pick it up. Flying that airplane up through Canada and then into Alaska was a great experience. The scenery along the trip was amazing and the weather was great, it being summer. I began to put the airplane to use in ministry and the extra room was working well.

The next spring, in April, I had to make a flight down to another village. This village was roughly 250 miles to the southwest. After spending the night in the village I prepared to head back home. It was a clear day and the weather was expected to stay good all day. This should make for an enjoyable flight back to the family, I thought. After departing the village, I climbed up to a thousand feet above ground, set the controls, and headed home.

I was just starting to cruise along when I noticed that the power setting was coming down. I figured I must not have set the lock ring tight enough to hold the setting, so I added power and retightened the ring. In less than a minute, the power setting started to come down again. Immediately, I began to examine the gauges to see what was going on. It didn't take long looking because the engine came to a sudden grinding halt. The propeller stopped, and as I looked, black smoke was pouring out from the engine, coming out through the cowling. I'm not a mechanic, but I knew this was not good.

Without even having to think about it, my response was "I need ANRC." I set the plane controls to try to get the best glide out of it, which gave me the ability to cover more ground. Hopefully, this would give me good landing options. At the time, I was flying over some tall spruce trees, and I knew I didn't want to land among the trees. To the west lay the river, so I turned the plane in that direction. Aviate and Navigate were now taken care of. Resuscitate was the next step, which was simple. There wasn't going to be any restart on this engine. I moved onto the last one while I continued to head toward the river. Communicate was next. I keyed the mic and said, "Mayday! Mayday!" Then I provided my airplane data with my current location and my intention.

Fortunately another pilot responded. His first question was whether I could restart the engine. If he was in my seat, he would realize that's not going to happen. I once again gave him my information and location and told him that I was about to crash. I made it over to the river, which had no trees and was still frozen. That was the good news. The bad news was that the river had a few feet of snow. My airplane was not equipped with skis; it had tires on the landing gear. The snow would soften my crash, but it would also be a problem for the gear. As I came silently gliding toward the river, my new landing strip, I said a final prayer.

I have a friend who was in an airplane crash earlier. After impact in the trees the airplane had caught fire. He was severely burned, but he survived. My prayer before I crashed was, "Lord, please don't let me burn like my friend." One of the reasons for my concern stemmed from the fact that I had three five-gallon jugs of avgas strapped right behind me in the backseat of the plane. After clearing the trees and turning the plane downriver, I tried to keep a smooth, steady approach leading to the landing. I could feel the plane touch down on the snow. Then it all happened so fast. The next thing I knew I was hanging upside down. I unbuckled, reminding myself not to fall on my head. Once unbuckled, I worked to get the door open and then crawl unto part of the wing and then step out on the snow. I was alive, unhurt, and there was no fire.

I looked at the airplane: one gear was ripped off, both wings were bent and twisted, and the tail section was bent. I walked away from the airplane a short distance, still fearing a fire. One pilot knew where I was and was heading my way. Afterward, I found out that the two missionaries in the two closest villages had also heard my mayday call. They had called the mission office to inform them of my crash, not knowing the outcome. The office then informed my wife, who also didn't know the outcome. She was reassured of being informed as they got further details.

There was one missionary located on the river where I crashed. They quickly formed a search-and-rescue team and headed my way. I only stood on the snow for half an hour before I heard the snow machines coming. As we worked on getting the plane upright to drag back to the village, the airplane that heard my call flew over. I was thankful he had responded, yet grateful that the village men had already come. After working our way back to the village, I was able to call my wife and let her know I was okay. The plane was a total loss, but I was so grateful that God kept me safe. The little bruising and soreness were nothing in comparison to what could have happened.

As I thought about that crash, I knew the training I received about "ANRC" was crucial in my survival. Again, it was grilled into me so much that it was a part of my being. Paul encouraged Timothy to study the Word of God, that he might be a workman for him (2 Timothy 2:15). I do not think Paul was suggesting a casual reading, but rather an intense study—perhaps to the point that he would know the Word of God so well that it would become a part of him. When God called Ezekiel to be his spokesman for the people, God told him to consume a scroll (Ezekiel

2:8–3:2). That scroll was the very words of God. That is an incredible reminder to me. Do I know the Scripture as well as I know ANRC? Knowing the ANRC saved my life, yet how much more do I need to know the Scripture for my spiritual life? Are the words of God a part of me? Do I know the Scripture so well that regardless of time, place, or subject, I will be able to share God's Word? May I rise to the challenge— it will save my life in the end.

PLAY BALL!

It was another hot, humid, summer day—typical for this time of year in northwest Ohio. My mom looked at me from the kitchen sink where she was doing the dishes and asked me where I was going. I quickly responded that I was headed to the ball field, fearing that if I didn't hurry I would be late. Swinging the door behind me and jumping on my bike, my legs began pedaling quickly. Unfortunately, the ball field was on the opposite side of town. It was one and a half miles to the field, but pedaling would be a good warm up for the game. Starting with little league, then all the way through high school, this scenario repeated itself countless times. Playing baseball was a passion of mine. Defense was my game and I loved to play outfield, particularly left field. It was always exciting to snatch a ball from the sky and send the batter back to the dugout. Offensively I was horrible, but my defense kept me in the starting lineup.

As always, life changes. It was off to college, then onto a career, marriage, and a family. Suddenly, or so it seemed, baseball was out of my life. There was no time or opportunity for me to play "the game." Then on our first year in the village as a missionary, when summer arrived, I found out that the men played fast-pitch softball. There was now a slower pace to life and I was going to get back in the game. Around thirty years had passed since I first stepped onto a ball field. However, I could still run and throw the ball, so back to the outfield I went. The softball was a lot bigger than the baseball but that was not the only thing that was different.

I was used to standing at home plate, bat ready, watching the pitcher deliver the ball overhand. However, in fast-pitch softball, the pitcher delivers the ball underhand. The ball was still thrown in such a way that you had to watch as the ball moved side to side or up and down. The ball may come to the plate slower than a baseball but the pitcher was closer to the batter. The batter had to read the pitch and react to it, as it all happened quickly.

The village was small in comparison to where I grew up. Ten thousand people is quite different than a few hundred who lived in a village and call it home. Despite the small size, people would gather at the ball field in the evenings. Some would come to play, and others to watch and visit. The women would normally have their game first followed by the men. Many a times the men's game would start around midnight. One of the blessings of living in the far north country is the summertime sunlight. With darkness being postponed until late summer, the game could happen any time of the day or "night," as it is always light outside.

There was one thing that was the same—whether the game was played during my childhood days or here in the village later in life, it all came down to competition. The games were played with intensity, especially when it came time for tournament play. It seemed almost every "night" the teams would play, all in preparation for one of the village tournaments. During a tournament, the surrounding villages, from roughly a hundred-mile radius, would gather together. The teams would travel by boat on the river or come by airplane. The tournament would last over the course of a weekend with almost a dozen teams, both men and women, competing for the championship trophy.

Throughout the years I had competed in countless tournaments. The years were beginning to add up and now I was playing at first base since I was no longer able to run fast or throw far. The good thing about first base was you didn't have to run and others throw the ball to you—all you had to do was touch the base and catch the ball. The adjustment went well and I came to enjoy playing first base. As usual, late in the summer, the tournament was going to be played in our home village. Though I was well into "elder" status, being over sixty, I was eager to play the game. The teams arrived, the competition began, and I was intent to do my part to try to help our team win the event.

During one of the games I stepped up to the plate and managed to get a single. While standing on first base, I began to think about trying to steal second. Sure enough, the opportunity came and I ran fast and hard for second—that is, as fast and hard as an old man could run. But everything came together and I beat the throw to second. Safe. There are moments in life when we sometimes get a little delusional. I was now having one of those moments. As I stood on second base I began to think about stealing third. Watching the pitcher, I started leading off. I was trying to get a good lead, yet not so much as to get picked off by the pitcher. I started off the base, keeping my eye on the pitch, then the opportunity came. The catcher bobbled the ball and lost it behind him and I was on my way to third base. But then it happened.

I heard the stories. Older men shared some lessons with me from their own experience. Apparently I had not been listening. Standing a little distance from second base while watching the pitch and the catcher's mishandling of the ball, my mind immediately told me that I could steal third base. My mind told me I could run faster, yet my body refused to follow the instructions between second and third. My legs could not keep up and I went tumbling onto the dirt. Again my mind kicked into overdrive and I immediately realized that it would take far too long to get back up on my feet and still make it to third. The solution? The only option I had—crawl the short distance to third base. With all the speed and grace I could muster, I crawled to third. The small village crowd erupted—some with cheers and others with laughter—but I was on third base. I was safe! Dusting myself off, and with my reason returning, I looked at home plate and said to myself, "No way!" At the end of the tournament I was voted as one of the "All Tourney Players." Everyone agreed that I was the fastest crawler on any of the teams in the tournament. This was a very vivid and visual demonstration that sometimes the mind says one thing but the body says another.

This principle not only applies to the game of softball but to life, as well. The apostle Paul wrote about the struggle between the mind and the body, the spiritual nature and the sinful nature. In Romans 7:15–25, Paul wrote that this war rages within us. In our mind we know what we ought to do. We know what spiritually is right; however, sometimes we fail. The body, our eyes, our ears, our mouth, all respond to the sinful nature—even though we know better. Sin rears its ugly head. Paul wrote in verse 15, "I do not understand what I do. For what I want to do I do not do, but what I hate I do." Again in verse 19 Paul wrote, "For I do not do the good I want to do, but the evil I do not want to do—this I keep on doing."

In Galatians 5 in verses 16–17, Paul wrote further on this topic. "So I say, walk by the Spirit, and you will not gratify the desires of the flesh. For the flesh desires what is contrary to the Spirit, and the Spirit what is contrary to the flesh. They are in conflict with each other, so that you are not to do whatever you want." This war that rages within us is a battle we fight even on a daily basis. How can we ever win this battle? How can the Spirit within us win over our earthly sins and desires? Perhaps by being completely immersed with Him.

Trying to steal third base was a stretch—in some ways I fell short. Yes, I made it to third, just not so gracefully. Similarly I struggle spiritually. Yet by God's grace the Spirit will rise up within me, and moment by moment the Spirit within me will win. As I spend time with Him in His Word, in His presence my battle will grow fainter as the Spirit within me grows stronger. Then one day, as I stand in His presence, I will have complete victory.

Power of Wind

It was just a small two-seat airplane—nothing more than a sling where two people could sit side by side. Some tubing with fabric covered the fuselage, wings, and the tail, yet it was an airplane…and it was my first airplane. Almost full throttle on a good day would get me eighty miles an hour. It was small and slow, yet it was the plane that helped me in ministry. I only had the airplane for two years before getting a bigger plane, but during those two years there were many flying adventures.

One summer we headed in for our annual mission conference. The conference was a great time of fellowship with other missionaries, as well as a time of receiving Bible teaching. Our mission's airplane was going to bring in my family for the conference while I flew my little airplane. Since my plane was slow, it was close to a five-hour ride from the village to the mission field office. Halfway during that flight, I would stop at a bigger village and refuel the plane. This summer day when we were heading into the conference, the weather was predicted to be windy.

Leaving the village early in the morning, I headed south. The first leg of the flight went great; however, the wind was picking up as I landed at the larger village to refuel the airplane. After refueling and taking a small break to stretch my legs, I took off and headed east. This part of the flight was going to be straight into the wind. What compounded the problem was that I was going through the Alaska Range, a large stretch of mountains arching through the southern part of the state. During this flight I would be winding my way through a mountain pass and flying from the west side of the mountains to the east side.

As I flew closer to the mountain range, the wind picked up. Slowly my plane went from eighty miles an hour to around forty miles an hour at ground speed. That was slow! But the worst was yet to come. Flying east, and with each mile getting closer to the mountains, the turbulence began to increase. I worked the flying controls rapidly and tried to keep the plane straight and level. Finally, as I headed into the mountain range, the wind became so strong and the air so rough that I struggled to keep my feet on the rudder pedals. My legs were being thrown off the pedals and up into the bottom of the instrument panel, which didn't feel too good. Fortunately, after I went through the top of the pass and started down the other side, the turbulence and wind backed off. The remaining flight to town was uneventful.

It is amazing how strong the wind is—it's a force to be reckoned with. After I moved up to the Cessna 180, I flew my son to the city for college. This plane had more room, more power, and more comfort than the previous airplanes I owned. Again, it was forecasted to be strong winds the day of this flight. As we headed out to the airfield, there were strong winds. The local weather station reported winds around fifty miles an hour on the ground. After getting the airplane loaded and ready, I taxied out for departure. With wind this strong, all I needed to do was point the plane into the wind, add a little power, and I would be airborne.

We departed the village and started to climb up for some altitude. Knowing that this would be a little slower and longer flight, I put on eighty gallons of avgas. Normally the flight would be two hours, but with heading into the wind I was prepared for a much longer timeframe. If the wind was fifty miles an hour on the ground, I knew it would be much stronger with altitude. As I was climbing, gaining altitude, my son did the usual college thing—he went to sleep. After climbing up to 5,500 feet, I leveled off the airplane and continued in my easterly direction. After twenty to thirty minutes of flying, I looked back and could still see the village behind me, which was not a good sign. I looked at my GPS;

it indicated a ground speed of twenty-eight miles an hour. My plane normally flew at 142 miles an hour, which meant that the wind had to be going over 110 miles an hour against me. I never experienced such strong wind before.

Doing some quick calculations, I realized that at my current fuel-burn rate and the given speed I wouldn't even make it to the next village, let alone the city. I woke my son up and told him to look behind him—he saw our home village and then I explained to him how strong the wind was and the fact that we would never be able to complete the flight. I pulled the power setting back, turned the airplane around, headed west, and let the wind take us back home. Making a big circle around the village, I finally lost enough altitude and landed back on the airstrip. Again, just as the wind made for a short takeoff, likewise, the wind made for a short landing. Taxiing to the parking spot, we tied the airplane securely to the ground anchors and went home to try another day. It's hard to imagine, but the wind was too much for the airplane that day; the wind held too much power.

The power of wind is reflected in Scripture, which displays the power of God. God used the wind to drive back the waters of the Red Sea so that Moses and the Israelites could cross over on dry ground (Exodus 14:21). I have seen the wind stir the water on the river, making some big waves, and there have been times when I have hauled a load of firewood back in my boat and wondered if I would make it. The wind was so strong and the waves so high, I feared the boat might be swamped—but nothing even close to the power of parting the waters.

Looking back in 2 Kings 2, there is the account of Elijah and his successor, Elisha. The time of Elijah's ministry for the Lord was coming to the end, but the Lord had a man to follow behind—a man who would continue to proclaim the truth. As Elijah and Elisha were walking along the road, suddenly a chariot of fire and horses of fire separated the two. Then the Lord took Elijah up to heaven in a whirlwind. I have seen the results of tornadoes and the damage that comes from that funnel cloud. I can't comprehend what the whirlwind that Elijah experienced was like. In any event, the power of God was once again displayed through that event.

The Lord appeared to Elijah as recorded in 1 Kings 19:9–11: "There he went into a cave and spent the night. And the word of the Lord came to him: 'What are you doing here, Elijah?' He replied, 'I have been very zealous for the Lord God almighty. The Israelites have rejected your covenant, torn down your altars, and put your prophets to death with the sword. I am the only one left, and now they are trying to kill me too.' The Lord said, 'Go out and stand on the mountain in the presence of the Lord, for the Lord is about to pass by.' Then a great and powerful wind tore the mountains apart and shattered the rocks before the Lord, but the Lord was not in the wind." It is hard to comprehend the power of that wind—a wind so strong that it tears rocks apart. But again, the power of the wind demonstrates the power of God.

Then we come to the day of Pentecost. The disciples gathered in the upper room to pray. "Suddenly a sound like the blowing of a violent wind came from heaven and filled the whole house where they were sitting. They saw what seemed to be tongues of fire that separated and came to rest on each of them. All of them were filled with the Holy Spirit and began to speak in other tongues as the Spirit enabled" (Act 2:2–4). The time of Pentecost and the coming of the Holy Spirit are described like that of a violent wind—a wind that had such a roar to it that you knew it was coming with power. We must never lose our understanding of the power of the wind. We must never lose our understanding of the power of God. And we must never lose our understanding of the power of the Holy Spirit. Let us walk in His power today.

Pray that Your Father Will Hear

It was a beautiful day to fly. The sun was shining brightly, and the air was still. The trip upriver to another village should be a good flight. I hoped this trip would be one that helped build relationships and trust with some of the people upriver. I fueled up the plane and performed the preflight. The floats had been pumped out and most of the water went back in the lake from which it had come. Each time I pumped out the floats, I wished a couple of the float lockers didn't leak so bad. But it was good exercise each time I worked the hand pump emptying the water out of the floats.

Before leaving, I stopped by to visit my elderly neighbor to see how he was doing. As I approached his porch, we began our conversation. He wondered if I heard the news of what happened upriver throughout the night. He told me a man had fallen out of a small aluminum boat and the river current took him downstream, and they had yet to see him at this point. He knew I was going upriver and told me this story for a reason. I assured him that I would search the river as I drew closer to the village.

As I flew along, heading northeast, I had a feeling of helplessness. What are the chances I could find the man? Even more, what are the chances that the body would even be in a setting where it was visible? I began to pray as I flew along and asked the Lord to help me find the body. I knew I could not do this on my own; I needed the Lord's help. I knew my help would build relationships and trust with the people. As I drew closer to the village, I intently followed the river at a much lower altitude. Following every bend while looking down, I searched the water closely. Fortunately, it was summer and the water was a little lower and clearer at this time of year. I was twenty miles out but saw nothing. At fifteen miles out, still nothing. The current was stronger in this region as the river was flowing through low mountains.

When I was eleven miles from the village, the Lord directed my eyes to a little spot on the river. The water was making ripples in one spot where all around there was none. The ripples seemed out of place at that location of the river. I decided to take a closer look. I circled around and flew closer while I still watched the hillside and the trees along the river edge to stay a safe distance from obstacles that may cause a crash. I began to look with new intensity; there it was—the abnormal ripple. I flew over the location and then I saw it—a tennis shoe and part of a jean pants. I circled again, but this time to land the floatplane close to this spot where I saw the articles of clothing. I began having mixed emotions stream through me. The family will be torn apart with the tragic loss of one of their loved ones. Yet the Lord answered my prayer in a mighty way and for that I was very grateful. I knew this would carry with it open doors—open doors that could lead to the sharing of the gospel of Christ. After landing and securing the plane to the bank, I waded out to the spot. I reached down into the water and began to bring the lifeless body to the shore. A boat I spotted earlier was making its way downstream. We loaded the body carefully and respectfully into the boat for the trip back up to the village. The family in the village would be grateful the body was recovered, yet now the pain and hurt would begin.

The Lord clearly called my wife and myself to bring the gospel to the people in the northern part of the interior of Alaska. As I worked my way back home, my faith was again challenged, and yet also bolstered. John 15:16 came back to my mind: "You did not choose me, but I chose you and appointed you so that you might go and bear fruit—fruit that will last—and so that whatever you ask in my name the Father will give you." The Lord had truly heard my prayer and had answered it in a mighty way. Unfortunately, this was not the last time I would have to lift up a prayer before the Lord, asking for His help in finding a body.

Fall was slowly transitioning into winter. The river was beginning to freeze along the edges, but most of it was still open water. As winter approaches, the water begins to drop, causing the ice on the edge to angle downward toward the lowering water level. One evening as the rain slowly fell, two young men were cruising around on their snowmobile. The little snow that was on the ground made it possible for them to make their way around the small village. These young men were drawn to the river since it's a "highway" for travel and a way to provide food for the table. These two men had intentions of traveling the edge of the river; however, as they tried to turn on the ice and head upriver, the slope and slippery surface from the rain prevented that turn. Their snowmobile slid off the ice into the dark, cold water. Immediately realizing their peril, the older individual pushed the younger one onto the ice and then he disappeared into the darkness of the water. His life had been given to save another.

The village is a small, isolated, and tight-knit family community. Word of the accident traveled quickly via phone and marine band radio. People quickly gathered at the riverbank. Unfortunately, even after hours of searching, the search had to be called off due to the darkness and the ever-present danger from the shore ice. The next day, men searched from boats all-day long and dragged the bottom of the river back and forth but yielded nothing. The women on the bank were there for support and to supply food for the searchers. Darkness came and, again, the search was halted. Hearts were heavy as we again left the bank and headed back to the village.

The next morning broke with clear skies. Before the search began, the chief of the village wanted me to lead the prayer at the church before we began searching for the day. The church is just a small log building, but everyone squeezed into the structure and I began to pray. I prayed for safety for the searchers in the boats and comfort for the family and the strength to continue on. Then I prayed, "Father, I am asking you to help us today. Lord, help us to find the body today."

The rest of the day went exactly like the day before—men dragging, women supporting, and no body. I was working in one of the boats and saw the sun sinking down and drawing close to the horizon, so I said a silent prayer. "Lord, I asked you for your help. I asked you to help us find the body today. I believe you can do this. This community heard me ask you, so for your glory, help us find the body." Our boat with the three occupants made another pass, then back again. Suddenly one of the men said he felt something on the drag. Slowly he pulled the drag up, and as it got closer, I saw the body of the man. I reached down into the cold water and grabbed ahold of the lifeless body. With help from other men we put the body into the boat and took it to the shore. We gathered together, standing as one on the riverbank as an elder offered a prayer of thanks unto the Lord.

God had indeed answered the prayer in the waning light of the day. The village proceeded forward with the grieving, the "burial," and, in time, some healing.

I am being reminded what an awesome God we serve. Prayer is so often forgotten, yet so powerful. Why does it seem that I call on the Lord only in seemingly desperate situations? Rather, I should be more attentive to remember what is taught in 1 Thessalonians 5:17. I know that God hears my prayer. I know that God will answer my prayer. Lord, help me to pray.

STAY ON THE TRAIL

S ome say that winter lasts a long time in Alaska. If seven months is long, then we have a long winter. But with the winter comes some great activities. One of the more interesting activities is dogsled racing. The famous Yukon Quest runs for 1,000 miles between Fairbanks, Alaska, and Whitehorse, Yukon. Then there is the Iditarod—a race of 1,000 miles between Anchorage and Nome. But these dog races are not the only ones in the state.

Every winter over the Christmas holidays, our little village has a variety of sled dog races. Men's and women's, and even children get into the races. This particular winter I was going to race in the Old Timers' race. For two years I qualified to compete in the Old Timers' race, but my son-in-law couldn't convince me to enter. Yet this year was going to be different. One day my son-in-law walked into my workshop and said straight out, "You will be racing with eight dogs on the six-mile track. The race starts at 1 o'clock, so be at the starting line." He turned and left—possibly with a hidden smile. Finally, on the third year he had put me in the Old Timers' race.

Race day came and I was at the starting line. I was bundled heavily because of the cold. I walked up to the race marshall and informed him that I had never raced dogs before and was happy to go last. He clearly stated that all the racers were going to draw cards for race positions and I would be expected to do the same. "Okay," I said, "but I would be happy to draw last." I figured if I drew last out of the six racers, then maybe that would help my odds to start in the back of the field. In time, I took the last card and I turned it over—it was the ace of spades. I would be starting first.

I helped walk the dog team up to the starting line. The eight dogs were jumping at their harnesses, eager to run down the six-mile trail. I had no idea where that trail went through the woods so I was hoping it was marked well. My son-in-law is a man of few words. There was so much that I didn't know about racing and he hadn't communicated anything to me. Right before the race marshall started the race and as I was standing on the sled runners, my son-in-law walked up to me and said, "A little way down the trail there is going to be a hard-right turn so be ready, so you don't get thrown off." He then walked off and my mind wondered, *What is a "little way"?*

The dog handlers were holding onto the race sled on each side with all their might to keep the dogs from starting too soon—all the while the dogs continued to jerk on their harnesses, yelping with eager anticipation. The final ten-second countdown unfolded and the dogs jerked—the race was on. Immediately, I felt the wind in my face and made sure my boots were securely on the sleds runners. I began to watch for that hard-right turn. It came soon enough. I leaned into the turn, slid around the corner, and glided into the straightaway. I began to relax and thought the rest of the race should be easy. I started enjoying the scenery and the stillness of the woods. The only sound was the glide of the runners on the snow, and even though the dogs were working hard, running for sheer delight, they were quiet.

The trail was easier to see than I thought. Obviously, it had been dragged by a snowmobile. As I was making my way through some stands of birch timber with scattered jack spruce trees, I suddenly noticed an old faint trail crossing mine. I was glad the trail had been dragged and that the dogs would know the trail from previous runs. Without warning, and for some unknown reason, the lead dog made a ninety-degree turn to the right onto that faint trail—and the rest of the team followed the lead dog.

It happened so quickly, plus with my lack of experience, I was totally caught off guard. Suddenly, the dogs were going in one direction while the sled, with me on it, was going in a totally different direction. Then the sled jerked to the right from the force of the dog team and I proceeded in the direction of the main trail—minus the sled under my feet. As I got up from the snowbank I watched in disbelief as the dog team, with the empty sled, headed rapidly away from me.

Instinct took over and I yelled at the team—I can't remember what I yelled, but surprisingly it affected them. The lead dog turned back toward the trail I was supposed to be on. A huge wave of relief washed over me as I witnessed the team coming back. But the relief was short-lived. I realized that the team was going to enter the trail fifty yards up from where I was standing. This elder was no longer "sprint material." Not to mention I had a lot of clothes on to keep me warm. Between age and clothing, swiftness was not in the picture. However, I gave it a gallant effort. I tried to run and meet the dogs where they would reenter on the trail. As I watched in despair, the team ran down the trail. At this point they should make great time now that they were minus 180 pounds.

Earlier, before the race began, the race marshall had stationed men around the six-mile course at various locations. I figured that up the trail there would be a volunteer and he would probably hold the team for me. I began to alternate between running and walking, heading up the trail to catch my team. Of course, since I started first, and the other teams started at two-minute intervals, they were beginning to catch up with me. As some of the teams passed by there were a few comments made. One of the mushers watching me walking along the trail asked me if I lost my team—I wondered what his first clue was. Another musher wondered if I wanted a ride. Somehow a little macho pride came in and I said I was fine. I was starting to wear out as I jogged along, but I finally saw the volunteer with my team. He began to yell at me to hurry up. Unfortunately, at this point, there wasn't any more "hurry up" left in me. The volunteer lined out my team as I got back on the sled runners, and in a few seconds I was back in the race, though losing a few positions.

The dogs took off, pulling with all their might, and snow flew by as I cruised along. Unfortunately, it was a short cruising session. My son-in-law failed to mention another situation that might arise on the trail. The lead dog had a bad habit of abruptly stopping and squatting to…well, you get the picture. Wouldn't you know—he did it. This rookie racer wasn't ready for such an event and neither were the other dogs. I looked in disbelief as the dogs began to pile on top of the lead dog. I stepped on the sled brake, but not quick enough. I ended up on top of the dog pile. I pulled the sled to the side, set the sled hook to hold it securely in place, and looked at the dog pile I had to untangle.

Amazingly, after a few minutes I had the team untangled and lined out again, ready to go. Just as I was about to pull the hook, I saw a team coming up the trail. And here he came, the legendary sprint dog racer of all time. I was not about to take off in front of the musher who won more sprint dog races than anyone else. Once he passed, I unhooked, jumped on the sleigh, and took off. The dogs made amazing time. Of course, they hadn't worked too hard in the race since the sled was empty for a good part of it. As we neared the finish line I knew without a doubt I had claimed last place—but I had stayed on the trail and completed the race.

Scripture reminds us of the importance of staying on God's trail. God told Joshua to obey all that He had commanded and not turn to the right or the left. Proverbs 4:26–27 reminds us to watch where our feet go—keep them on the trail, not turning to the right or left. It may seem narrow, but it is right and is the best path for us. Why does it seem so easy for me to wander from what God has written? I realized quickly that I needed to stay on the trail for the dog race. How much more in life do I need to stay on God's trail?

THE GLORY OF GOD

The air is crisp and still as darkness comes upon the land. In the distance under the clear, starry night, you can see the silhouette of the mountains. The river slowly meanders downstream, reflecting the world above. We stand on the edge of the riverbank, gazing upon all that surrounds us. There are no lights from men on the horizon—silence is everywhere. But we turn around as the campfire draws us to its edge—the light, the warmth, and the crackling logs all add to its draw. From generation to generation this scene is played out. Within this setting is always the inevitable draw of campfires upon mankind—fire has a mystical draw.

For many in this world the setting is not the same. In the hustle and attraction of the world, men have lost the understanding of and appreciation for nature. Nature is a display of the glory of God. Could it possibly be that in today's world, we have shifted our focus more upon ourselves than on God Himself? On the other hand, if we are the ones who retain a focus upon the Lord, do we see Him as more of a friend than the great I AM? I remember growing up in a different time and a different way of thinking. When you would walk into church, although there are many people in the pews, you join them in silence. You gather together and believe you are standing in the very presence of the Lord. You are there in silence, in prayer, and in reverence.

Moses led the people to the mountain where God was to appear before them. On the morning of the third day, as the people stood at the foot of the mountain, there was thunder and lightning and a thick cloud over the mountain. Then it came—a loud trumpet blast. Everyone in the camp trembled, and as the Lord descended upon the mountain it trembled violently and the sound of the trumpet grew louder and louder. God came down on the mountain and Moses went up on the mountain to meet with God (Exodus 19:16–19). I can only imagine what it must have been like. What would it have been like to witness the sounds, to feel the trembles, and to see with your own eyes the smoke billowing up the mountain as your leader communicates with God? Is it any wonder that everyone present, without hesitation, trembled before the Lord? Though the people did not see the very glory of God, they were in His presence at the foot of the mountain, and that alone was enough to make them tremble.

At another time and another place and with another man, God had a message for His people. In Ezekiel 1:25–28, Ezekiel saw heaven open and saw visions of God. He saw what looked like a throne of sapphire. And high upon the throne was a figure like that of a man. From His waist up, He looked like glowing metal as if full of fire. From the waist down, He looked like fire. Brilliant light surrounded Him and His appearance was the likeness of the glory of God. Ezekiel fell facedown as he saw the Lord Himself, in all His glory—so brilliant that He could only be described as fire.

Summers are days of warmth; the temperature climbs to the 70s. This time is also the season of endless light. The sun shines in the sky for up to twenty-one hours a day. The days of cold and darkness are behind. These are the days full of hustle to once again prepare for the onslaught of winter, which will come all too soon. It was on one of these summer days when I was reminded once again of the brilliance of fire. As I was hauling avgas down to the floatplane to get ready to fuel it for a flight, the truck I was using suddenly quit. After checking things out, I realized there was water in the fuel. Water doesn't seem to want to ignite and burn in the engine like gas. With all the flying I had to do, the truck would have to wait until later in the day to get fixed. The sun was still shining as I landed back on the lake that evening at around 11 p.m. My wife and I went back down the trail to try to start the truck. I came prepared with a corn can, filled with clean unleaded fuel. My plan seemed simple and straightforward: I was going to put a little gas directly into the carburetor as we tried to turn over the engine. Lifting up the hood of the truck, I took the air filter off so that I had direct access to the carburetor. With my wife inside the truck, I told her to turn on the key once I put gas into the carburetor. The truck fired right up, but it only ran until it used up the gas I poured in. After two failed attempts to keep it running, I wanted to make this third effort effective. As my wife cranked over the engine for the third time, I poured a little gas into the carburetor. Immediately the engine caught but began to die as it burned up the fuel. I didn't want it to stop again so I quickly poured more gas into the carburetor. The engine caught, but as it continued to sputter there was a sudden backfire. Flames shot up out of the top of the carburetor, immediately catching on fire the gas I had been pouring out of the corn can. In a panic, I tried to quickly remove the can from under the hood of the old truck, but unfortunately I bumped the can onto part of the truck. I threw the flaming can onto the ground. As I looked in disbelief, the truck had caught fire. Not only that, the grass and weeds also caught fire when the gas from the can I threw had spread. Further, I looked down to realize I was on fire since some of the gas had spilled on me, too. In what seemed like a heartbeat, three fires were blazing—and it seemed they were getting out of control. My wife jumped out of the truck and told me to "drop and roll." We were able to extinguish the fire on me fairly quickly. Then we turned our attention to the truck fire and the brushfire. What kept running through my mind was the fact that if we couldn't control this fire then it would spread to the village. Fortunately, a couple of friends came by and helped us put out the fires. Yet in those brief moments, fire totally captivated my attention.

John, on the island of Patmos, also saw heaven open and gave us a picture of God on the throne. There upon the throne sat one like the son of man (Revelation 1:12–17). His head and hair were white like wool and

His eyes like blazing fire. His face shown like the sun in all its brilliance. John, upon seeing this vision, fell to his feet as though dead. This was the same response generated by the three disciples on the mountain with Jesus (Matthew 17:1–6). The disciples, upon seeing Jesus and witnessing that His face was like the sun, fell facedown upon the ground. The entire chapter of Revelation 4 is devoted to giving us a picture of God on the throne. The response of the elders, in the presence of the Lord, is to give Him praise and glory—and to fall facedown before the One seated on the throne. Everyone who sees the glory of God falls down on the ground before him.

If we consider the response of those who have gone before us, as is recorded in the Word of God, it would cause us to pause and reconsider what our response to the Lord should be. Our vision should not be so focused inwardly or horizontally, but rather more vertically. If we remember the descriptions of God given by the prophets—the ones where He is on the throne and is as brilliant as fire—we would fall to the ground and give Him glory. Even as we attend church, we would gain a clearer understanding of what church is about—it is not about us, but all about Him. It is a time of worship and of falling down before He who is on the throne. May we gather together and lift up the very name of the Lord and give Him all glory.

THE GREATER MISSION

"Why are you fishing for such a 'small fish' when you can catch big ones?" I was asked. Having my interest aroused, I inquired to see what they meant. I was fishing in some new territory and lessons could be learned from the local people, if I was willing to listen. As in all of life, there are lessons, even spiritual lessons, to learn if we will only listen—lessons that help us toward a greater mission. As I stood on the airplane floats, with the plane nudged into the bank of the river, I continued to have a conversation with some of the natives.

This fishing adventure had been months in the planning. It all started with a call from an old friend. He wanted to come to Alaska with his son to do some fishing. Of course, when the call came the land was a block of frozen ice. However, it was good to start the planning process early. A time that would accommodate everyone's schedule was selected, and I began to think about the various fishing opportunities the summer would present. Knowing some of the potential places to go and the great fishing that could be had, I did something I had never done before—I set aside five days from the work schedule and devoted this time to take my friends fishing.

We planned to go up a small river that was just above the village. I had made this trip many times and I knew from experience that we could get into some good pike fishing. The river trip in itself is a joy. There is always a challenge every time you stop the boat. Mosquitoes, for instance. It is amazing how fast they can find a human and are relentless in their effort to consume some of your precious blood. Swarms of the small pests descend upon you at every chance they get. But the good fishing makes it worthwhile, even to the point of enduring all the mosquitoes.

Another day would include a trip to a lake. But this is not just any lake—this beautiful lake is on the south side of the Brooks Range Mountains. It is clear, with a bluish tint to the water. The mountains jet up from the northern edge of the lake as a small river flowed just to the south of it. The flight there takes you over several valleys interspersed among the mountains, and each valley you cross gets you closer to the Arctic Circle. Trees are missing this far north. The climate is too harsh for them to grow, and therefore the visibility is unlimited, especially from a mountain ridgeline. With the lake nestled in this setting the scenery is breathtaking, and the fishing is great. This lake had provided some incredible lake trout fishing in the past and it seemed a good spot to revisit.

One day of the trip had been set aside to go after this small fish—a fish known as the grayling. This fish occupies the uppermost part of the river systems known as the headwaters. The water is almost always clear and swift in this setting. The fish may be small, but the locations are amazing. The plan was to fly into a small lake that bordered the headwaters of a small river to the north, and from the lake we could walk over to the river and start fishing. It's always interesting to be able to look through the clear river water and see the fish that you are trying to catch. A little spinner or a small fly, all presented in a manner to entice that fish to bite.

The day had come to try our luck on grayling. However, before we headed to go fishing I dropped my son off at a village so he could visit people he knew. That's when we had our initial conversation with the locals on the riverbank, who asked us why we would go for small fish when there are big ones to catch. After a brief visit with the locals, we changed our plans. We were now after a new quarry—sheefish—the big ones. I was told that if I flew upriver a few miles and landed where two rivers came together, then we would have some good fishing.

Pushing off the bank, piling into the airplane, and firing up the engine, I headed off for our new destination. After a short flight, I found the location where the two rivers came together. We landed on the river and slowly taxied up to the gravel bank. After securing the plane, it was time to try some fishing. Sure enough, no more had the spoon hit the water than a fish was on. It was obvious from the bend in the rod and the pull against the reel that these were sheefish, the tarpon of the north. The silvery body shimmered in the light as the fish jumped out of the water. Once landed, it was back in the water with the spoon. It seemed every time you placed the spoon in the location where the two waters came together, you had a fish on the line. Now this was fishing!

A grayling is impressive with its big dorsal fin. The state record is around five pounds. Though landing a five-pound grayling sounds exciting, sheefish fishing was proving unbelievable. The state record for sheefish is over fifty pounds. The size difference is dramatic. This was proving to be a greater mission. Tackling a fish of this size and with such frequency provided a real adrenaline rush. Fish after fish kept our attention drawn to the blending of the two waters. Unfortunately, the light began to wane and it was time to head home.

The sheefish adventure was a much greater adventure than the original mission of grayling fishing. Even looking at the ministry of Christ, one could get caught up in the daily events and lose sight of His greater mission. The crowds heard that Jesus was back in Capernaum and they entered the house where He was preaching. Many people gathered together and there was no room left in the house. Four men lowered a paralytic through the roof on a mat in front of Jesus. After a brief discussion Jesus healed the paralytic (Mark 2:2–12). This was not the only miracle Jesus performed during his earthly ministry. Remember the time he and his disciples were crossing the sea? A severe storm arose and threatened their very lives and the disciples pleaded with Jesus to save them. He stood up, rebuked the wind and waves, and immediately it became calm

(Matthew 8:23–27). These and the other miracles were a testimony to the fact that Jesus is the Son of God. However, were the miracles the ultimate reason for Christ's coming? Was this His greater mission?

Jesus began His ministry at around the age of thirty, and He ministered for almost three years. In his brief time on earth there was one driving passion, one central focus. Jesus talked about this passion and focus in John 12:27: "Now my soul is troubled, and what shall I say? 'Father, save me from this hour'? No, it was for this very reason I came to this hour." Christ's ultimate mission was to die on the cross—to shed His blood and to provide payment for our sins, that through Him we might have eternal life. This was His reason to come. This was His greater mission…and He accomplished it.

What about us? What is our greater mission? There are many grand and noble undertakings and accomplishments that we can focus on. We can pour much time and effort into various goals, but what is the number one goal we live for? What should be our focus and our driving passion? If all else fails, what is the one thing we want to accomplish in this life? "So whether you eat or drink or whatever you do, do it all for the glory of God" (1 Corinthians 10:31). "And whatever you do, whether in word or deed, do it all in the name of the Lord Jesus, giving him thanks to God the Father through him" (Colossians 3:17). "If any one speaks, they should do so as one who speaks the very words of God. If anyone serves, they should do so with the strength God provides, so that in all things God may be praised through Jesus Christ. To him be the glory and the power for ever and ever. Amen" (1 Peter 4:11). Jesus Himself said in John 15:8: "This is to my Father's glory, that you bear much fruit, showing yourselves to be my disciples."

It was easy to make a switch from a small fish to a big one. Christ was focused with one ultimate mission: dying on the cross. May the Lord help us to focus in this life on the greater mission: to bear fruit that brings Him glory.

TRAILS

I stood in the Colorado campground, surrounded by mountains, looking at the man. "I don't really believe all that Bible stuff," I told him. "I'm not really interested in God and I really don't want to hear what you have to say." I had stopped that day to check out their camp, making sure they complied with all the federal campground rules. This particular family caught my attention as there were quite a few children. The family was on vacation from Oklahoma, getting a chance to enjoy the mountains and also the cooler temperatures than summertime Oklahoma afforded. Just so happens, their dad was a preacher. As we were visiting, once the opportunity presented itself, I had shared with him my thoughts about religion.

The Oklahoma preacher looked intently at me. Maybe he was thinking about how young I was, but how confident I thought I was. Whatever his thoughts, with firm words he began to share the gospel message with me. Intent upon making the message clear and forceful and yet sprinkled with grace. After he had spoken for a while I stopped him, and with a small smile I informed him that I was only messing with him. I, too, was a believer. I loved the Lord and I just wanted to see what he would do if I pretended to be against the Lord and His Word. That unusual conversation was the beginning of a relationship that lasted forty years, even covering most of my time in Alaska.

Years later, as I was flying along the Brooks Range of Alaska, my eyes were moving from one panoramic scene to another. This range of mountains is farther north than any other range in North America. It is huge, it is majestic, and it is remote. Looking out the plane window, I could see that some of the hillsides were solid red as the fall colors of the plants were on display. Rugged peaks jutted up toward the blue sky. Clear streams of water flowed in the valleys below, rushing for the ocean. This piece of earth below me also held some of the greatest concentrations of caribou, noticeable especially with the coming of fall migration. The herds would be moving from the flat tundra on the north side of the Brooks Range, coming through the mountains and on to their winter range farther south.

Caribou are always wandering. Just their walking speed is something that men struggle to keep up with. But at this time of year their wandering has a purpose. They are moving south before winter takes its grip upon the northern tundra. There will be thousands upon thousands upon thousands of caribou making this annual migration. Though they wander aimlessly at other times of the year, this trip is different. As I continue to fly along, the sides of the mountains are marked with their distinct trails. Trails that were made a long time ago, but still followed today. For in this migration the caribou will follow behind each other. Usually an older cow will lead the way with the others following behind in her step. Even in winter you can see the caribou strung out single file as they make their way through the snow. One will make the trail and the others will follow.

One of the last times that I saw my preacher friend from Oklahoma was in a small church down in southern Oklahoma, while we were doing some visiting in the lower forty-eight. It was a Wednesday evening fellowship time. There was a great meal, singing, and then a time of sharing from the Bible. Someone from the church came along beside the old preacher, helped him up out of the pew, and then helped him make his way up to the pulpit. He was frail, but finally up front he sat down on a stool, opened his Bible, and began to teach the Scripture. The crowd was small, but I doubt that mattered to him. What mattered was the clear teaching of the Word. "Friend, I want to tell you something…" thus would be the beginning. Even though he was almost ninety years old, his heart was to still proclaim the truth. He wanted to impart upon us the very words of God. A man after God's heart, walking with him and serving him till the end.

I had many opportunities to visit with this preacher through the years. Times were spent in his church office, in his log home, or back up on the mountains in Colorado. He would always bring the conversation to things that mattered the most. "How is your walk with the Lord?" he would ask. This older man became my spiritual mentor. He had been down the trail of life further than me and he understood and saw things that I wasn't even aware of. Yes, he had been wounded in WWII. Yes, he had lost part of his left arm. Yes, some would say he was handicapped. He wouldn't. Despite his injuries his passion centered around the things that mattered the most in life. Things of the Lord. Nothing was going to keep him from proclaiming the truth, not even some old wounds. He led by example and he marked the trail for others to follow. He was that mentor for me as I followed behind him on the trail of life and on my journey with Christ.

Scripture records the stories of many who have gone before us, those who have served as examples for us to follow. Remember the time of Moses. The Israelites complained against God, they complained against Moses, and they complained about their circumstances. Moses cried out to God for them. What an example of a pastor's heart—one of compassion. During the time of Joseph's life, he was unfairly sold into slavery, unfairly accused by a woman, and unfairly put into prison. When he became leader, he judged justly. What an example of truth and grace. After Stephen shared the Word of God before men and before the Sanhedrin, they began to rail against him. As he proclaimed the truth, they proclaimed that he had spoken heresy. He stood before them with the Word of God and he knelt and prayed for them as they were stoning him to death, and then he fell to the ground asleep. His dying breath spent praying for his persecutors. A prayer of forgiveness.

Paul in 1 Corinthians 11:1 reminded the people to follow his example just as he followed the example of Christ. What a blessing for the believers to have someone to follow, whether it is someone from the Scripture or someone with us today. Whether it be Paul, or whether it be someone like the old preacher from Oklahoma. But that raises a question. If it is such a blessing to follow someone who has already set the trail for us, who are we setting the trail for and what kind of trail?

Whatever age we are, wherever we live, whatever we do, someone is watching us. They watch the way we handle situations. They listen to the things we talk about. They will not just listen, but they will see how we live life. What are the things that we focus on? What consumes us? Where do we really stand with the Lord and how much is he really a part of our life? Sure we might go to church on Sundays, but what about the rest of the week? Is he truly our Lord and Savior? Or do we just talk the talk when it seems appropriate?

This now becomes a huge challenge for me. Can I rise to the occasion to be a godly mentor for those around me? Can I make a trail for them to follow that will be an upright and godly trail? Can I be like the ones who went before me in Scripture, or can I be like that old Oklahoma preacher? Even the caribou knows the importance of making a trail, of leading the way for others to follow. The challenge is there. Lord, give me the wisdom, grace, and strength to leave a godly trail for someone else to follow.

WE LOST IT

"What do you mean you lost it? How could you lose it?" My wife's questions were coming quicker than I could answer.

"Well, it's not exactly like we lost it," I told her. "I mean, I know where it is." I proceeded to explain in clearer detail what I had discovered.

It was fall, which meant hunting season. Once again the search was on for food, particularly moose. I traveled fifty miles by my little john-boat up a small river into one of my favorite hunting areas. Once there I set up camp. I gathered some firewood into a pile, set up the tent, put up some meat poles, and made a fire pit. The weekend hunt, although enjoyable, produced no moose. I knew I would be hunting this area throughout the season since it had proven productive in the past. Therefore, I decided to leave my camp setup, along with some of the supplies, throughout the season.

Toward the end of the season, after being unsuccessful in harvesting a moose, I decided to venture up the small river back to my camp. After traveling the winding river for a couple of hours, enjoying the coolness in the air, I rounded the bend for camp. Things looked different on this trip. The leaves had mostly fallen off the trees and the migratory birds were generally all gone. I tied up the boat to the steep bank. Then I saw the damage. The tent, although partially standing, was torn to shreds. Not only was the nylon tent ripped apart, but bent pieces of metal tubing were lying at odd angles. Apparently, a bear decided to see if there was anything worthwhile in the tent. I hadn't left anything there, but he still investigated and left me a trashed tent. Just like I told my wife, I didn't really lose the tent...but I lost the tent. This event made me think back to an account given in Scripture.

The order had been given and there were no options—the order must be followed: you do not go against the king without serious consequences. Little did it matter if the king was but the age of a boy. The priests and others were at work, repairing and cleaning the temple. Perhaps because of the boy's lineage, this was important work to be done. In any event, the temple was being renovated. Then unexpectedly, they found something of great importance—a book. But not just any book. This was the missing book of the Law. It contained the writings of the ancient prophets. Here was not just the history of the Israelites, but also the history of God and the account of creation, the flood, and the exodus. This book contained accounts of God dealing with men. All of this within one book—this was the Word of God.

This book, although missing for years, was now back in the hands of men. Did everyone understand how important this book was? Perhaps not. But most would soon as word of this great find quickly spread up the ranks. Then in due order, the king was informed of its appearance. "King and royal majesty, we have found the book of the law."

The order of the king was clear and direct. "Bring the book to me and have it read in my presence." Once he heard the reading of the book, the king tore off his robes. He knew the Lord's anger burned against them because they and their fathers had not been following what was written in the book. Thus, the king made a new directive: gather all the people together because this book, which was lost, was now found, and it would be read in the presence and hearing of all the people.

How long did it take to read the book? I can only imagine that it was a lengthy process involving a considerable amount of time. But it was done, nonetheless. It had been read in the presence of all the people, and at the end, the king challenged the people to follow everything that is written in the book—this book, which is the Word of God. The people, in one accord, committed to follow the king's request (2 Kings 22–23). They committed to follow everything written in the book of the law.

What about us today? We have not lost the book…but have we lost the book? We live in a chaotic world. Long gone are the simple days—rather than one rarely leaving their home state, most travel between countries with ease. Airplane travel a few decades ago was only for a few; however, now it is the norm. Party phone lines, which were the norm, have been replaced with personal cell phones. Long gone is black and white television—UHD was not even understood back then. Much of life was around the family farm, and many families hardly ever moved away. Now we are a society of movement. Technology made rapid advances and finances improved and adjustments were made to accommodate all these changes. People changed, too. And time has become a precious commodity.

I remember when I was a young kid growing up in Ohio. One of my fond memories was going to visit my grandparents. In my early years they lived on a farm, but in time moved to a small town. I remember going to their home and spending time with my grandpa. What big hands he had—those worn hands put food on the table for the family. He made a way in this world. Every time I walked into their home, one thing never changed: there on the side table was their family Bible. It was a huge Bible full of pictures. And at a young age it captivated me. I would sit on the couch, slowly turning the pages, and look from one picture to the next. There was too much print on the pages for me to even think about reading it, but that book held a special place in my life.

Today there are other Bibles in someone's home—maybe even in your home. It could be sitting on the table, on the nightstand, or in a drawer. But it is there. It is the Word of God, just as it was during the days of Josiah. And it's the same as it was during Josiah's day—the book is being unused because it is lost. Maybe in our house it is being unused, but not because it is physically lost, but because we have lost the passion to read the Word of God. In our head we know that this is His word. His message has not changed and it will stand forever. It is for us, but maybe we are not interested to hear what He has to say. Maybe everything in life consumes us, even our time, and there is nothing left for His Word. Or perhaps we have gained worldly knowledge but lack the desire to learn godly wisdom (2 Timothy 3:7). We have concluded that His Word is important and gives us instruction for life, yet we will go it alone because we rely upon our thinking, our understanding, and our direction.

Obviously, Josiah had a different perspective regarding the Word of God. As a people, he said, we are not just going to read the Word of God; we are going to follow His commands. The challenge lies for us then—to not just pick up the Bible and read it, but obey God's commands. Perhaps this is part of the reason why we fail to read His word. If we don't read it, we won't know His standards and then we won't have to conform our lives to those standards. How much easier is it if we can live as we think? But just as Josiah knew there would be serious consequences for not following God's Word (2 Kings 22:11–13), so it will be also for us. We need to find this lost book, blow off the dust, and read it. But not just read it—follow the commands that are written within the book. Then in our lives, what was once lost will be found.

WHAT GUN NOW?

Subsistence. It's not about sport; it's about survival. Living off the land and harvesting what God has provided so that we will see another day. I heard stories from the elders of ones who in the past had not made it to another day. Hardships had come, cruel reality had set in, and the end result was death—death by starvation. Today it's not so dramatic, but the necessity to harvest from the land is still a vital part of life in the bush. Through the years I was learning more and participating in this subsistence lifestyle. Fortunately, I had lived and hunted in Colorado in the past, which had helped prepare me for living in the bush. It also provided me with the opportunity to secure a variety of guns. This at least would allow me the opportunity to select a good caliber gun for whatever quarry I might be hunting.

It was early spring. There was still plenty of snow and travel by snowmobile was good. The sun was shining for fifteen hours and the days were getting longer. There were no more days with only three hours of light. The temperature was in the upper twenties and that seemed incredibly warm after having seen winter temperatures of negative fifty. Early in the spring as the temperatures rise, it will cause the snow to melt a little. Then with the night and colder temperatures, the snow freezes and forms a crust. This crust makes it easy for traveling by snowmobile. This allows men to move about the land, for these were the days you could explore new country and learn from the surroundings. Trapping season was now over, but it was a great time to look for caribou. These animals never came close to the village but they would migrate within our travel range. One of the men coming back to the village from a caribou hunt spotted some tracks. These, however, were not ordinary tracks—they were fresh grizzly bear tracks. The wind had not yet blown snow into the track, so it was still distinct and soft. Apparently, the bear had just come out of his winter den and he was on the move. Once the guy made it back to the village and shared the news of his discovery, it didn't take long for word to spread. Men began having conversations and making plans for the following day.

Early the next day a group of men gathered at a local house, finalized a plan, and headed out of the village. I came, equipped with my .45/70. The bear would probably be in the timber, so the shot would be close and maybe in thick brush. The open sights in this situation would be better than having a gun with a scope on it. This also seemed like a good caliber to me and the lever-action gun had proved effective in times past. The .45/70 may be a slow bullet, but it has a lot of weight and punch. We left the village and the men spread out, looking for fresh tracks. Soon enough tracks were spotted and the hunt began. After a few hours we spotted the bear and one of the men was able to harvest the animal—the hunt had been successful. Eliminating one of the major predators of moose meant the survival of more moose. It is amazing how many moose are lost each year to either wolves or bears. After the hunt, the men regrouped together in the village. Another hunt was planned the next day to take advantage of the good weather.

I pulled up the next morning to the same house I was at the previous day. This time we were loaded for a long trip. The birch basket sleighs were packed with the necessary supplies for the hunt: survival gear, food, guns, extra clothing, and game-processing equipment. Today we would be traveling roughly 120 miles round-trip on our snowmobiles, looking for caribou. As I pulled up to the house, the owner had noticed I had a different gun. He mentioned that the gun I had was only a single shot. He was right; however, I knew from experience this was an accurate gun.

There would be a good chance today that we would be shooting a long distance. Accuracy would be more important than a large quantity of bullets, different than the day before. I wouldn't be too interested in facing a grizzly bear with just a single shot. Yesterday the gun had open sights, but today the rifle had a good scope.

We left early in the morning knowing it would be a long day. There were five of us going out on three snowmobiles. This was going to be a great adventure for my two oldest grandchildren. The trail was well marked but rough, which put the snowmobile suspension to the test. After taking some rest breaks along the way to enjoy the nice weather, we finally reached the area where the caribou had been migrating through. This group of caribou were slowly working their way back north, heading back to their summer range. Finally, we spotted some caribou and began to position ourselves to intercept their path of travel. The terrain was wide open and the distance was long, but I was confident in the gun. After working ourselves into position we waited and watched. When the time was right I placed the gun across the snowmobile seat, using it as a rest. After four shots there were four caribou on the snow. This was enough meat for our family with extra meat to hand out to some of the elders. In this area of the state we are permitted to harvest five caribou a day, but there is only so much room in a sleigh to haul the meat back. It had been a good hunt and the single shot .30-06 had performed as anticipated.

We had two different days, two different hunts, and two different guns. There is a reason why there are different calibers of guns and different kinds of gun. Each gun and each caliber was made for a specific hunting situation, depending on the game that is hunted. No one gun can fit every situation because there is not a "one size fits all" in the gun world. Each caliber and each gun uniquely fills a specific need. Given the setting we live in, everyone in the village has multiple guns to meet the many scenarios of hunting we encounter.

Likewise, that is how it is in the church regarding believers. God made each one of us unique. He gave us a specific build, a personality, and certain abilities. In the same way, when we became a follower of Christ He gave us specific spiritual gifts. He gave us the gifts He wanted us to have (Hebrews 2:4). Each gift is important, and each gift is needed (1 Corinthians 12 and 13). The church is not at its greatest potential unless the individuals within the church are using their gifts. See 1 Peter 4:10; it teaches us to use the gifts that we are given. Somehow, we tend to think that certain gifts are more important than others. We mistakenly focus upon these few gifts, ignoring the other gifts. The result is that the body is incomplete because important pieces are missing. Sometimes we may even become jealous that we don't have a certain gift. We forget we are gifted of God, for His purpose and for His glory. The greatest challenge for us is to be actively participating in the body of Christ and use the gift that He has given us, and help bring the body to the fullness that He intended. Lord, help me use the gift you've given me, for your glory.

WHERE'S HOME?

"Is it always this cold? I can understand it being cold outside, but I'm not outside. Why is it so cold in your house?" Those were questions I heard more than once. But like any good story, it all started years earlier.

We were excited to move to the house on the other side of the sandy road. The one we were currently in was okay and had served a good purpose for us, but the other one would give us more room. The first house we lived in for two years was less than 500 square feet, so the added room of the new rental would be appreciated by my wife and three kids. Moving day arrived and with great anticipation we carried all our belongings across the sandy road, over to our new rental house. The move was easy because we only had to carry our belongings a hundred feet.

This new rental was one of the original log homes built in the late fifties, when our village was started. It was located close to the river, which afforded us a great view. Upstairs we divided one of the bigger rooms into two with a curtain. Now the boys could have one room and our girl the other room—communication was still easy between the curtain. It would also prove interesting as the kids would have to go through our bedroom to get to theirs. However, this was going to be a better house for us with all the added room and more than doubling the size of our previous house. We unpacked everything and began settling into the new house.

Memories were quickly made in this new setting—not just family memories, but also ministry ones. The village kids were a constant part of our daily life. We also held both the junior and senior high youth groups in the house. There were times of playing games, Bible lessons, and fun and visiting. One of the great memories involved the senior high youth group. One evening after we had finished the lesson and were starting the refreshments, one of the young girls made a funny comment about being white. I quickly went into the kitchen area, reached into the flour bag, and went back into the living room. As I approached the young girl, I mentioned that she could also be white. With white flour flying through the air she immediately took on a new complexion. My wife was very gracious as her living room was transformed in front of her eyes as the flour fight began.

Time took a toll on the old log house. It was approaching forty-five years old with no real upkeep done throughout the years. The log walls were starting to bow and the lower logs were starting to rot, and the ants were helping to break down the logs. With this deterioration it wasn't as airtight as it used to be. Thus, in the winter it became more of a challenge to keep the house warm. One advantage was we had a huge built-in freezer; we could set things on the floor in the back room to keep them frozen. In the living room, although the woodstove was operating, frost would still form on the wall behind the couch, which was just twelve-feet away. Memories were made.

Our landlord began to encourage us that it might be time to build our own house. At their suggestion, I began to make plans to build a new log house—a log house all our own. Winter came and with it I travelled to an area where there was a large stand of spruce trees. House plans were drawn up and I knew about how much timber I needed to complete the project. The first step was to ring the trees, taking a section of bark off the trunk around the tree. This step would kill the trees. Each year when winter came, I made a trip out to the wood yard and checked to see how the standing trees were drying after having died. After three years I decided it was time to begin harvesting the dead trees. I spent two winters hauling the timber to my mill in the village with a snowmobile and sled. During those two summers, I began milling the timber into four-sided logs. Other parts of the logs were milled into boards that would be used during the construction process. As we went through each winter in the old log house, we looked forward to our new house.

After two years, the milling was done and the construction could begin. It is always an amazing process to see a pile of material turned into a structure. With help from some individuals, the house began to take shape. I labeled all the logs as they were milled, so each one had a specific location. The construction process, though started, would take a long time until completion. The ministry within the village needed to continue. Building a house was secondary. With time, effort, and money the project was completed. After two years of labor, early one spring, we moved into the new house. Thirteen years in the old log house had been memorable, but we looked forward to making more memories in the new house.

It was a rewarding experience to stand in the new house. The process took seven years, but it was finally complete. All the work of gathering the material off the land, starting with standing spruce trees, now ended with a house—a house that, with my wife's touch, turned into a home. It was our home for almost twelve years. Then after spending nearly twenty-seven years in the village, the Lord called us to a new ministry and a new location. We moved to the road system. This was going to be a huge switch—the bush to the road. The Lord was gracious, and we found a nice log home to buy, even with some acreage. One fall we made the move and, once again, set up our new home on the road system.

We are no different from most in society today. Life is filled with transitions—a new job, a new school, a new location...the list can go on. All of this transition may bring about uncertainty, but it also brings excitement. What will our new life be? Where will we live and what will our new home look like? These transitions are a good reminder that things in this life are temporary. Even friends, although we can't envision it happening, will come and go. Locations that we once dreamed of living in become distant memories. Houses that we invested our time and money into become empty buildings as we move to the next location. Life is full of temporaries. Yet there is something that is permanent.

Home. Not our earthly home, but rather our heavenly home. Jesus said in John 14:2–3 that He is preparing a place for us—that is our heavenly home. In Revelation 21:1, John said that he saw a new heaven and a new earth. These are destined for eternity. As a follower of Jesus Christ, I have this promise of a new home where I will spend eternity with the Lord. We are reminded in Philippians 3:20 and 1 Peter 2:11 that our real citizenship in not in this world, but in heaven. We may be proud of our earthly citizenship but it pales in comparison to our heavenly citizenship. What can our temporal, earthly home have to offer us in comparison to our heavenly home?

Looking back at the saints who have gone before us, we see we are led by a great, godly example. Hebrews 11:13–16 reminds us what our priorities should be. Here is a picture, a telling, of men and women who have walked the trail of life. They realized that they were not truly citizens of this world because this world was not their home. They lived their lives looking for a better citizenship. They dreamt of having a better home. They were focused on heaven and its home. Their eyes were looking up for they were not dwelling on the past or the present—they were looking to the promised future.

What about us? Is this the attitude we possess? Are our hearts set on things above rather than things of this world? I will pour out my life to build a home for my family, one that will rot and fall to the ground. But will I pour out my life to lead my family to a home that is in heaven, one that will last for eternity? I must face this question. Where is my home? And what home am I leading my family toward?

WORK IN PROGRESS

The village lifestyle is subsistence. You live off the land and this brings with it some challenges. Much of your time is spent making sure that you have what you need to make it through the next season or the next year. But this lifestyle also has some advantages. People are more important than things, and within that framework comes the attitude of taking time to visit. Through visits you find out what is going on in your village and in the surrounding villages. You also hear what is going on with fishing, trapping, or hunting—depending on the season. Whatever is important at the time is passed on during these visits. The visits also pass on traditions and stories from the past.

My neighbor was an elderly gentleman who was good at telling stories. Whatever the topic might be, he had a way of weaving a good story into it to make it interesting. Often I would wander over to visit and quite a few times I got to hear many of his stories. One of the stories that he talked about from the past had to do with boats. Since I enjoy working with wood, these stories always drew my attention. He would start talking about how they used to make wooden boats.

"Today, most boats are made commercial and they are made out of aluminum. Before that boat material came about they used to make boats out of plywood. However, back in the day, they used to make boats out of spruce." He would pause, take a sip of coffee, and then the story would continue. "In the springtime, after the snows melted, some of the men would get together. They would look for a spruce tree, cut it down, and then begin to whipsaw that tree into boards. No chain saws or mills—it was all hand-tool work." As the story unfolded he would begin gesturing how the men worked with the tools. "The tree they selected had to be straight grain and best if it didn't have a lot of branches. All of that would help make for a better board. Once they had the boards cut for the planking, they would begin to make the necessary pieces to form the ribs of the boat. After they had all the ribs made they would begin to put the planks over the ribs. Finally completing that process, they would seal the boat joints with pitch from a spruce tree." Almost an expression of joy would come across his face as he was reliving the past, seeing in his mind the boat being built. "Of course, as the wood would get wet, it would swell some and help make the joints waterproof. When all was completed they would have a boat that would serve them well for the summer season."

Through the years I heard my neighbor describe this process over and over. He would tell me that in some ways a wooden boat was better than an aluminum boat. Of course, the aluminum boat would hold up to rough treatment and the weather wasn't such a factor. But the wooden boat would float better, turn better, and was quieter in the water—not to mention the satisfaction of making the boat by yourself, from the materials you gathered off the land. After some years of listening to the boat stories, I decided to give it a try. I asked my neighbor when the last time was that he could remember someone building a spruce boat. He thought for a while and then told me that on this river no one had built a spruce boat since the late fifties, as best he could remember. Knowing how long ago it had been, since the fifties, it gave me extra incentive to build a boat out of a spruce tree.

The project started with pencil and paper. As I traveled around to different villages, I would see an old plywood boat sitting on land, collecting water. Although it wasn't spruce, I knew that some of the angles and dimensions would still apply. I would record the measurements on a piece of paper. After collecting all of this information, I then began to draw up some plans for a boat that would meet the needs of my family. It then proceeded from paper to gathering the needed materials.

Since it was now winter, it would be a great time to gather some dead spruce trees off the land. These trees would give me the material I needed to make all the dimensional lumber. While on my snowmobile I would find a tree, cut it down, and then haul it back on the wood sleigh to the village. Just as I had been told, I looked for a straight grain tree with fewer branches. By the time spring rolled around I had gathered all the trees that I would need to make the boat.

Summer found me fighting the bugs while ripping boards out of the trees on a sawmill and bringing them to my wood shop. This was going to be a time-consuming project. I knew it would be a work in progress over a few months. Eventually, the mill work began—ripping, cutting, and planning the rough-sawn boards into dimensional lumber was all part of the process. Once I had made these boards, which would serve as the planking, I began to tongue and groove the edges. This would allow the boards to fit snugly together, giving more gluing surface. Most of the boards were only three to four inches wide. The best boards were set aside to make the ribs. After some work, it was time to begin putting the ribs together. Once completed, the planking boards were screwed in place over the ribs. Sure enough, in time, as the planking was added, it actually began to look like a boat. I knew now why the elder got an expression of joy on his face as he relived the boat-building process. I couldn't help but get excited as the boat slowly took shape. Once all the planking was done, I fiber-glassed the outside to seal up the wood. Paint was applied as a final coat and then I had a finished product.

Details, details...and then more details. Yet each one was important, and they had to all follow a certain order for the boat to become useful. If you skipped one step there was a good chance that the boat would not work properly. Time consuming? Yes. But the end product was worth it. There before me was a spruce boat, made from the land, and it would serve me well for years to come. When I first looked at the tree in the woods, who would have thought that it would end up as a boat? But by putting forth time and effort, a handmade boat was on the river—and the elder was right: you can't beat the way a wooden boat rides!

As I was working on the boat, I couldn't help but think how this must be like the Lord working in our lives. He takes some rough material and turns it into something amazing. It is a process and it will take time. There will be some effort put forward. But we are a work in progress. Just like the wood when it is first broken into pieces, so also we need to be broken. It may take something in our life to get us to that point of breaking so that Christ can begin the work (2 Chronicles 7:14). But we need to understand that apart from Christ, we are nothing. We need Him in our lives, for He is our only hope.

Just like us, the disciples needed to be broken so that Christ could do the work. They were unschooled, ordinary fisher men (Acts 4:13). Yet the Lord called them to be followers of Him. Reading the gospel accounts, one realizes this is an ongoing process. The Lord spent three years with these men. He ate with them, walked with them, He performed miracles in front of them, and He taught them. At the end of three years, He then told them to go into all the world and make disciples. They had been in the presence of the Master. They had been shaped by the Master. And now they were equipped to do the will of the Master. Many of these disciples died fulfilling the command of Christ.

Likewise, Saul, the one who was persecuting the Christians, would be touched by the Lord. His name would be changed to Paul. However, more than just his name was changed—he was changed on the inside and used as an instrument of the Lord for the furthering of the kingdom. This change would be brought about through trials, troubles, and persecutions. This man, this work in progress, came to become one of the greatest witnesses for the Lord in troubled times. He, too, like some of the disciples before him, was killed for his faith. Yet despite this, he was shaped by the Master and left his mark upon the world.

What about me? If I am a true follower of Christ, am I willing to let the Potter mold the clay? (Isaiah 64:8). Am I willing to be changed into a useful instrument for His kingdom, regardless of the cost? Do I understand that this will be a work in progress? Just as a dead tree was made into a useful boat, am I willing to be made into something useful to the Lord? Will I allow the Lord to begin His work in me?

WORLD OF WHITE

The brown color was about to disappear. With the beginning of winter, the coming snow would change the landscape. No longer would there be the barren trees or the dead grass covering earth's floor. Instead the land would become a world of white. Snow would begin to fall with tree branches hanging onto some of the white flakes. Others flakes would fall slowly, landing on the dead vegetation. The landscape, once drab, would now take on a whole new dimension. White, with all of its shadows and swirls, would become the new standard for the next seven months. A beauty all to its own—and so remarkable. The simple color of white transforming the quiet setting and making this new world.

It is a quiet world. The ducks and geese are gone, along with the swans and cranes. The caribou are moving to their winter range, farther to the south. The dens that were empty are now occupied by the bears, their openings covered with grass. The beavers are now in their houses, venturing out only to swim beneath the ice and living off their cache of greens. The songbirds that filled the air have wandered south to the warmer-climate zone. A few animals still move through the woods. It is a different world now. With the quiet comes a feeling of serenity and stillness is now the norm. It almost seems as if the world is at rest—no noise, no movement, just a world of white.

The engine roared to life. The silence was broken as the 300-horse-power engine swung the three-bladed prop around at 1,000 revolutions per minute. We were going to let the engine run awhile and give it time to warm up before we started to taxi down the ramp. I was taking two missionaries down to a village a couple of hundred miles south of our home. They were making a trip around the interior of Alaska to visit with some of the village missionaries. I checked all the instruments; everything seemed good. We made our radio call and headed for the runway. Pushing the throttle in for full power, we slowly gained speed as the runway lights began to whisk by—we were airborne.

I had mentioned to my two passengers the night before that I wanted to get an early start for our flight down south. The weather service was forecasting that a major snowstorm from the southwest would be heading into the state by late morning. Looking at my time after liftoff, it looked like we would be okay. Beating this big storm was a priority. As we flew along, looking out the window, it sure didn't look like a storm was coming. The sky was clear, winds were calm, and visibility was unrestricted.

It is always interesting to watch landscape change after flying so many miles. Some areas are mountainous and void of vegetation, while other areas are flat with timber covering the landscape. The flight was enjoyable, watching the changing scenery and visiting with the passengers. However, after almost an hour and a half of flying and as we drew closer to our destination, I could see the coming front of the storm. The blue sky gave way to a distinct cloud line that looked ominous. Looking at the map to determine the distance to the village, I could tell this was going to be close. Shortly, I looked over to my passenger in the copilot seat and let him know that we were not going to make it to the village before the storm hit.

We were now within twenty miles of the village and drawing closer to the storm. What would the last fifteen miles be like? How intense was this storm? After thinking through the options, I turned to my friend in the copilot seat and gave him my decision. "We are within ten minutes of the village and we're going to fly into the storm. We're going to try to make it to the village." Some decisions, when you look back afterward, you wonder how you ever reached them. This could be one of those times. The storm front looked like a wall and we were getting ready to enter that wall.

I turned the airplane slightly to the east and positioned myself along that bank of the river. On the western side of the river was the village, but there were also the mountains and I wanted to be over the flatland on the eastern side. I began to fly along the riverbank, down low, keeping the tree line just off the left wing. As I flew into the storm reality hit home quickly. The leading edge of this storm was intense. There weren't a few flakes floating down, and then in time a gradual building in intensity—no, it was immediate. There was a reason it looked like a wall. As I flew along the tree line I looked to the west, across the river, trying to spot the village. No such luck. The village lay one mile away, but the house silhouettes couldn't even be seen. After flying several miles downriver, my GPS indicated that I was below the village. I decided to turn around and come back up the river, staying along the bank on the east side. I was grateful for the tree line, which gave me some guidance as I was flying.

When the GPS indicated we were straight across from the village, I made a ninety-degree turn and headed west, flying across the frozen river. Leaving the tree line behind, which was my only point of reference, I saw that there was nothing but white. Somewhere out there ahead lay the village. The river was white with snow, the sky was white with snow, white snow and everything around us was white with snow. There was no determining what was up or down, right or left. Becoming spatially disoriented was now a possible reality. This is one of the leading factors of plane crashes. At this point, if one relies upon instinct, one will make the wrong decision. In this situation the only reliable way of maintaining a correct flying attitude is to trust the instruments—only the instruments will lead me safely to the village. Shortly, as we flew along, the vague images of houses appeared on the horizon. We were going to make it to our destination. The instruments were right while my instincts would have been wrong and fatal.

The realities in this flight can also relate to the realities in life. "There is a way that appears to be right, but in the end it leads to death" (Proverbs

14:12). Is this true? If we follow our own thinking regarding salvation, does it lead to death? Is there only one way for salvation? This topic comes under much scrutiny, discussion, and speculation. However, just assuredly as you will crash in whiteout conditions if you don't follow the instruments, so also you will fall short of salvation if you don't follow what Scripture teaches. So what is it exactly that Scripture teaches regarding salvation?

Jesus said in John 14:6: "I am the way the truth and the life. No one comes to the Father except through me." To follow Christ and become a disciple of His means coming to the cross, understanding that we are sinners, and that there is nothing we can do to save ourselves. It is only through the shed blood of Christ on the cross that our sins are covered. He gave His life so that we may have life, and He paid the price so that we may experience His grace. It is a coming to repentance, faith, and trust in the Savior, Jesus Christ, and believing that when we put our faith and trust in Christ alone, that we become a new creation. The old life is gone and new life has come. We are children of God and He is our Father. We have the Holy Spirit living in us and the promise of spending eternity with Him (Romans 3:23, 6:23, 10:12–13; 2 Corinthians 5:17).

Flying through storms in Alaska is not an uncommon experience. It can be done, but it is not an enjoyable activity. If I could have a choice, I would take the nice, clear, calm days to be my flying times. It is always enjoyable to watch the scenery go by as one cruises along with no worries about weather. Likewise, one can make it through this life without the Lord, but it is not the most enjoyable. In the long term, it does not lead to positive results. Just as I trusted in the plane's instruments to lead us safely to our destination, we, too, must trust in the Instrument of Christ Himself for safety and security in salvation. Why not follow God? Why not go through life with Him by your side, in the pilot's seat? Why not follow His trail and His way—and enjoy the ride for this life and eternity?

You Got a Sharp Knife?

The birch leaves were shimmering in the breeze; their yellow color seemed to reflect the sun. It was a beautiful fall day and we were headed back to the village. That morning had been a successful hunt. Noon found us with the moose all cut up, stowed in game bags, and now in the front of the boat. Despite the weight of the meat and the family, the boat was still moving along at a good rate of speed. About halfway home my son-in-law asked me if I wanted to stop and take a walk back to a grass lake and look for a second moose. Grass lakes may have a little water in them, but mostly it is just three or four feet of tall grass, which provides good food and a great bedding area for moose.

The boat came to a gentle stop as it slid onto the sandbank. We anchored our boat to shore, grabbed our rifles, and headed into the woods. The gnats were really bad that year so the rest of the family took shelter in the boat cabin. After walking a short distance, we came to the edge of the grass lake where we had seen moose in the past. Glassing the area didn't reveal anything. We didn't hear anything, but we decided to do a couple of moose calls to see if there would be a response. After a couple of grunt calls, and a little raking, a bull moose walked out. The moose was toward the end of the grass lake, so we headed in that direction.

Once we worked our way into range I was able to knock down the moose. One moose is a lot of work and now we had the second. The good thing was to know that the freezer would be filling up with meat for the year. Walking along the edge of the meadow, we came to where the moose fell. I will never forget what my eyes saw next. The gnats were so bad this season that the downed moose's hide appeared to be moving. But it wasn't the hide—the moose was covered with so many gnats that as they were crawling on the hide; it gave the perception the hide was moving. What an unbelievable sight! However, we now had to start the process of getting this moose cut up.

There on the ground lay around 1,500 pounds of animal to process. But that would not be the greatest challenge—the greatest challenge would be to deal with all those tiny little gnats. These little bugs try to get in any opening they can find. It could be a loose sleeve, an opening around the neck, up into your nose, your eyes, or your ears. They are relentless, and once they find their target, they bite. The gnats would be bad enough on any sunny, warm day, but the problem was compounded by all the gnats on the moose. As my son-in-law and I looked at this sight we realized the gnats now had two more warm bodies to attack. Specifically, these two warm bodies were close by; they weren't moving much and they weren't going away for a while. This would be a great day for the gnats and a tough day for us.

There is nothing a guy can do in this situation but dig in and get the job done. We needed to focus on taking care of the animal and try to ignore the gnats, which were already attacking. We were ready to skin out the animal once we got it on its back. The hide on a moose is thick and has long coarse hair. My son-in-law asked me, "Do you have a sharp knife?"

Knowing the size and the toughness of what we would be cutting, I always carry several sharp knives in my pack. "We have sharp knives," was my reply. We wanted to make the process as fast as possible given the conditions—this was not the time for a dull knife.

Every fall before hunting season, one of the rituals that I go through is to make sure every knife is sharp. Once, one of my grandsons had received a knife as a gift, and since he was young at the time he was excited. One of the first things he did was to check if the knife was good and sharp. He had watched his dad and me check our knives, so he did the same thing. Unfortunately, he maybe hadn't watched closely enough. He took his thumb, and instead of running across the knife's edge he ran it down the knife's edge. As the blood started appearing on his thumb, he immediately knew his new knife was sharp.

Opening my pack sack, I grabbed a couple of my sharp knives and we then began cutting the moose. Normally after we skin the moose we end up cutting the carcass into eight or nine pieces, depending on the size of the animal. This process normally takes us around an hour to cut and bag the meat. The gnats were relentless, and several times while cutting the moose we had to stop and run out into the grass lake. We just needed to get a little fresh air and try to get a little break from the gnats. Even if it was just a break for a minute, we were grateful. Once the meat was cut and put in game bags, we went back to the boat.

Packing the meat to the boat was only a few hundred yards, but at least we were moving, which helped slow the attack of the gnats. Once the meat was in the boat we resumed our trip back home. While on the river we opened the cabin doors and blew the gnats off us and the family that had been waiting in the cabin. It was a great feeling to watch the gnats disappear as we cruised down the river. The ride home would be enjoyable and gnat-free. Once we landed back at the village and began to unload the meat, the gnats would be there to greet us once again.

With the meat hanging up on poles, the smoking process begins. Smoking the meat entails burning cottonwood in a small fire under the meat. The good thing about cottonwood is that it smolders for a long time and normally there is not much flame but mostly smoke. There was a brief time of rest as we let the meat age before we started the cutting process. It was a good family time as we turned the big pieces of meat into small packages of steak, hamburger, stew and rib meat. Before that process began, all the knives were re-sharpened. And while we processed the meat, the knives would continually need sharpened. There's nothing better than a good, sharp knife when working with meat.

Swords are sharp, too. Back in the garden, the crowd came up to arrest Christ. Peter, always being the bold one, saw the threat to Christ and pulled out his sword, and struck the servant of the high priest. The sword was sharp, and the right ear of the servant was completely severed. However, Jesus kept the situation from escalating. He reached out His hand, touched the man, and healed his ear (Luke 22:47–51). Interestingly, during this miraculous healing, the crowd still continued to arrest Christ. Such is the passionate error of men.

In the book of Revelation there are a couple of pictures of Christ given by the writer John. In both descriptions Jesus is seen as having a sharp, double-edge sword in his mouth. John revealed in chapter 19 that with this sword, men who had followed the Antichrist and the false prophet would be killed by Christ. The sword is a powerful instrument used in the hands of the Almighty Lord.

There is another reference to the sword and its mighty power. Hebrew 4:12 says, "For the word of God is living and active. Sharper than any double-edge sword, it penetrates even to the dividing soul and spirit, joints and marrow; it judges the thoughts and attitudes of the heart." The Word of God is sharper than a sword, sharper than a knife—there is power in the Word and in comparison the words of men are as nothing. We should try to season our words more with the words of God. Using the Lord's words in our speech would communicate wisdom, grace, and power. Lord, help us to share your words.

THE FINAL MARKER

It was a Sunday evening in the middle of the church service. As I was preaching, I could hear snowmobiles rapidly pulling up in front of the church. A few people quickly entered the small log building that served as our church. It was obvious they were intent in their mission. Pausing in my message, I listened to what they had to say. They wanted me to go with them and tell a grandmother that her grandson had just been tragically killed. Closing my Bible, I quickly dressed for the winter temperatures outside and then proceeded on my snowmobile to the grandmother's house. Going into her house with the others, we shared the news of the death and then tried to comfort a broken, grieving grandmother.

It was another death in what is called "the winter of death." With a village of a couple hundred people, the last eight deaths spanning five months was enough to shake any community. Two of those deaths were natural, while the others were all of a tragic nature. In such a small, remote location, you know everyone who lives in the village. Each death not only impacts the family but the entire community. No matter the way of death, the outcome is always the same: a family is heartbroken. People gather at the home, to comfort and support the family. The days consist of cooking, digging the grave by hand, visiting the family, and gospel singing at night. Once again the men gathered at my wood shop and we began to make yet another casket. This year and in this season, the task became all too familiar. Along with the casket, a wooden cross was made, which contained words for the final marker. The basic process is the same in the lower forty-eight; however, the details will vary slightly. In the end, the last detail to be completed is always the final marker. This marker contains the name, the date of birth, and the date of death of the individual. Sometimes a short description is written on the marker about the individual.

At the least, at some point during the process there will be a time when people will say something about the individual. People will recall stories of something the individual did or perhaps something he had said. There is a mixture of laughter interspersed with the sadness of the loss of a family member or a friend. But from these words that are spoken, the family draws comfort—comfort from not just the comments, but also from the memories that the stories generate. However, quickly reality sets in for everyone involved in this family's loss. Life must go on—there is work that must be done and commitments that must be kept. Parts of the void that the individual left behind at their passing will shortly be filled by other individuals. There are parts of the void that can never be filled by anyone else. This causes me to wonder, *When our time comes and we die, what will people say about us? If they were to put something about us on our final marker, what would it say?*

Looking back in Scripture we see examples of those who have gone before us and what was said about them when they died. What is written about them is what represented their life—it is their final marker. Abel was commended as a righteous man (Hebrews 11:4). Enoch was one who pleased God (Hebrews 11:5). Noah was a righteous man and blameless (Genesis 6:9). Abraham was called God's friend (James 2:23). The list can go on and on. Throughout Scripture there is recorded a description of the people that could be put as a label on their final marker. Seeing these examples before me makes me wonder, *What will be on my final marker?*

Summer had come and with it a special Vacation Bible School (VBS) program for the kids in the village. This particular summer there would be a group of people coming from one of our supporting churches in the lower forty-eight. This group would lead the summer VBS program and it was always good to have someone else come to the village for this program. New faces, new energy, new format—yet all with the same message we had been teaching throughout the year.

The day arrived when the VBS would start. There was always a good turnout from the village kids for this program because it was something fun and exciting to do and the treats weren't bad, either. During the week, as the church group was leading VBS, one of the teachers made a comment about us as the local missionaries. One of the kids responded that they knew us—particularly me. Without much hesitation the little boy identified me as the "casket maker." Later that day, as we were gathered together around the supper table, reviewing the day's events, this topic came up. When I was informed of the little boy's description of who I was, it startled me. It was an accurate description of one of the things that I helped do in the village—but is this what I do most of the time? Is this all I'm known for? Does he not remember all the flying, or weekly kids' program, or Sunday service, or the other things I did to help around the village?

The little insight that was gained from the boy made me ponder, *What will people say about me when my time comes? When my life here on earth is done, what would people put on my final marker?* C. T. Studd lived from 1860 to 1930, and during those seventy years on earth, many of those years were spent serving as a missionary. Within his lifetime of experience and walking with God he came to pen a famous line: "Only one life twill soon be past, only what's done for Christ will last." What an amazing reminder regarding the reality of life! With that understanding, I needed to take time for reflection on my life. What will I do with that quote from C. T. Studd? Perhaps others need to reflect on their lives as I did. Perhaps these are questions all of us must ask.

Again, Scripture reminds us that this life is fleeting. "All people are like grass, and all their glory is like the flowers of the field; the grass withers and the flowers fall" (1 Peter 1:24). In another passage, Scriptures says, "What is your life? You are a mist that appears for a little and then vanishes" (James 4:14). Given that we only have one short life and that only the things done for the Lord will last, may we strive to have our final marker pointing to Christ.

What would God put on your marker? Would He say what He did of those men of old? Men whom He said were righteous, men whom He said pleased Him, men who were blameless and a friend of God. What would He write on mine? I am more than just a casket maker. What are things that stand out in my life? What is it that people see in me and recognize me for? Would people say that I am a man of God, or would they think differently? Perhaps there are changes that I need to make in my life, while I have the opportunity, to help form the words for my final marker. Perhaps we must all change our actions now to shape the words for our final marker.

CPSIA information can be obtained
at www.ICGtesting.com
Printed in the USA
LVHW081128250419
615482LV00007B/8/P

9 781400 306213